Finally FIGURED IT OUT

SHATTERING GENERATIONAL CURSES

A Journey from Brokenness to Healing

RHONDA HARRIS

FINALLY FIGURED IT OUT
Shattering Generational Curses: A Journey from Brokenness to Healing

Contents

PART I

PART II

First, I give honor to God—
The Author of my story, the Keeper of my soul,
and the One who never let go.
This book is my testimony of Your grace, mercy, and unshakable love.

And to my baby brother
You were my anchor in a world that never stopped shaking.
Though the silence you left behind is still
loud, your memory brings me joy.
You remind me that love never dies—it
lingers, it echoes, it carries me still.
I'll love you for the rest of my life, and I'll look for you in the next.

PART I

Introduction

There comes a time when silence becomes heavier than truth.

For years, I carried the weight of generational curses—chains forged in silence, shaped by fear, and inherited through generations. I lived through patterns of pain and survival that seemed impossible to escape.

Even in my own family, I often felt like I didn't belong. There was something different about me—something I couldn't explain. I wasn't better or worse. Just different. And for a long time, that made me feel isolated.

I tried to fit in. I tried to blend. But deep inside, I knew:

There had to be more.

There had to be healing.

There had to be freedom.

This memoir is more than just my story. It's a living testimony that generational curses can be broken. That cycles can end. That scars can become sacred. I am proof that you can be born into brokenness and still be destined for healing. That the cycle can stop with you.

Inside these pages, you'll find my truth—unfiltered and unapologetic. There will be laughter. There will be tears. There will be moments that might make you mad—and moments that make you see yourself.

I was born a boss—a fighter, a survivor, a leader. It took time, pain, and grace to figure it all out. But now that I have . . . there's no stopping me.

If you've ever felt stuck in cycles you didn't choose…

If you've ever longed for more than survival…

If you wonder if healing is even possible…

Know this: You are not alone. Healing is real. Freedom is possible.

Through God's grace, fierce determination, and relentless faith—I am here. And if I can rise… so can you.

Welcome to my story. Welcome to *Finally Figured It Out*.

Chapter 1

BORN INTO THE STORM: THE ROOTS OF MY FIRE

◇◇◇◇◇◇◇◇◇◇◇◇

"Even then, I didn't realize that survival wasn't the end goal—freedom was. And somewhere deep inside, I had already begun to search for it."

◇◇◇◇◇◇◇◇◇◇◇◇

Some people are born into love. Some are born into brokenness. I was born into a storm—and in that storm, a fire was sparked that would burn quietly inside me for years, waiting for its moment to rise.

I came into a world already heavy with history—shaped by choices and struggles that started long before my first breath. From the very start, the atmosphere around me carried both love and brokenness, laughter and pain. I was surrounded by people doing the best they could with what they had. Still, I often felt like a stranger planted in unfamiliar soil. Even as a little girl, I sensed something different deep inside me. It wasn't rebellion. It wasn't anger. It was a quiet knowing—a whisper that said, "You were made for something more."

In my family, loyalty was everything. I was raised to believe that blood was thicker than water—that no matter what happened, family sticks together. Family was supposed to be your safe place, your first home, your forever team. Those lessons were planted deep—spoken and unspoken—shaping how I saw the world.

In my family, loyalty wasn't just a value—it was a vow. "Love hard. Stand by each other. Forgive quickly. Never turn your back." It was spoken like gospel, passed down through generations like a sacred tradition. You didn't question it. You lived by it—or at least, you were expected to. Those words echoed through the walls of our home. You'd hear them in the middle of an argument, after a betrayal, or as a reminder when someone disappointed you. They were meant to bind us together.

But the truth? Sometimes they bound us to silence instead.

Because while loyalty was demanded, understanding was optional. While forgiveness was expected, accountability often went missing. And while we were taught never to turn our backs—too often we turned our hearts away. But even as I held onto those values, I wrestled with a truth that cut deep—loyalty didn't always mean understanding. Sticking together didn't always mean being seen.

I loved my family with everything in me, yet I couldn't escape the quiet ache that followed me like a shadow. It was the feeling of smiling in a crowded room but still feeling alone. The feeling of belonging by blood but not always by heart. I carried the weight of being both inside and outside—an outsider living within my own bloodline.

My early years were a mix of bright smiles and silent battles—moments of joy wrapped tightly around unspoken pain. I learned how to survive. How to shrink myself so others could feel big. How to go along just to get along. How to smile wide enough to hide the hurt burning inside. How to tuck away my dreams before anyone had the chance to crush them. How to carry burdens too heavy for small shoulders, and pretend they didn't weigh me down.

But even in the thick of it, hope lived. A flicker of light, the darkness couldn't snuff out. A whisper that told me there had to be more. And somehow, I believed it.

This is where my story begins—not in perfection, not in peace, but in the messy, complicated soil where seeds of healing were first planted. My childhood wasn't simple. It wasn't neat. It was a tangle of love and silence, of loyalty and loneliness, of bright smiles hiding bruised places no one wanted to name. But even in that chaos, something was taking root. Something inside me knew that broken ground could still grow something beautiful.

Growing up, I often wondered what life was like for my parents in the '70s—two teenagers trying to carve out space for their love in a world that wasn't always kind to young Black hearts. Their love was fragile and fierce, all at once—beautiful in its spark, but reckless and unprepared for the weight of real life. We—my siblings and I—were born from that love. Living proof of something raw, complicated, and still, in its own way, beautiful.

Every time my mother went to her six-week checkup after giving birth, she found out she was pregnant again. It happened three times in a row—her body barely healed before it was stretched again. Baby after baby, life piling up faster than she could keep up with. I can only imagine the exhaustion—the way her hands must have trembled from holding one child while carrying another inside her. The way hope and fatigue probably wrestled in her chest. Love was there, no doubt, but so was survival.

After a short break, she had my brother. Two years later, she had my baby brother—the one who would become the light of my life, the anchor I didn't even know I needed. He came into this world like a promise, like God saying, "Even in the chaos, I'll give you someone who will hold you steady."

That's where dysfunction quietly began for me. I was too young to understand the cracks forming beneath the surface—the exhaustion, the struggles, the pressures no teenage heart should've had to carry. All I knew was that love was loud and messy, and family was everything— but not always enough.

At the time, all I wanted was to feel safe, to feel seen, to know I belonged somewhere. But stillness made me uneasy. I didn't know how to rest in love that felt quiet and secure—I didn't trust it. I craved intensity. I clung to chaos. I mistook noise for connection. So I made drama out of peace, not because I wanted pain, but because I didn't know what peace looked like. Somewhere along the way, I learned to confuse love with survival. I kept choosing the fire because the calm made me feel invisible.

Now, looking back, I see my parents must have been overwhelmed. The love was there, but so were the struggles, the pressure, the im- possible task of raising so many babies while still being barely more than babies themselves. They were fighting to keep their heads above water—and in the process, I was learning lessons about love I would spend years unlearning.

At some point, a decision was made—one that scarred us all in ways we couldn't see at the time. My middle sister wasn't given up to strangers. She was given to my aunt to raise as her own. For years, we were told she was our cousin. We lived inside that lie, unaware of the truth that was shaping us in silence. And then, years later, the secret slipped. Someone revealed what had been hidden for so long: she wasn't our cousin. She was our sister.

That revelation shook me to my core. It left me confused, con- flicted, and heartbroken.

How could something so big, so life-altering, have been hidden? How could she have carried the weight of knowing she was the one who wasn't kept—while I walked beside her blind to her pain?

For me, it was shock and heartache woven together. Shock, because everything I thought I knew about my family was turned upside down in an instant. Heartache, because the people I trusted most had built walls of silence instead of bridges of truth.

That decision didn't just change her life—it changed all of ours. It left cracks in the foundation of family, cracks we spent years trying to step around without tripping. It taught me that secrets can suffocate love, and silence can scream louder than words. But it also taught me something else: that truth, no matter how long it hides, will not stay buried forever. And when it finally comes to light, it demands to be reckoned with.

Honestly, I still don't know why she was the only one. My parents never sat us down to explain what led to that decision—why she was the one they gave away and not the rest of us. Looking back, maybe I understand a little. Life can be unkind to children who aren't wanted. Too many end up lost in systems that don't love them, in places that don't protect them, in stories that end too soon.

Knowing what I know now, I applaud my parents for their choice. It was a decision born of survival—made from love in the only way they knew how. But what happened next planted seeds of dysfunction in my life.

When I was born, I came into the world an innocent child—oblivious to the weight already waiting for me. Without even knowing it, I had two targets on my back. Because of the gap left when one sister was given up, my mother made my oldest sister take me everywhere. Or rather, she forced her to. What might have looked like closeness on the outside was duty on the inside. That duty became resentment.

My oldest sister resented me because she felt like she was carrying a burden instead of a baby sister. My middle sister resented me because I was the one our mother kept after giving her up. Even as children, we felt it—an invisible current running through every interaction.

Everything shifted after that. The air in our home thickened with unspoken words. Hidden tensions rose like steam under a locked lid. The silent resentment grew louder with each year, until it was impossible to ignore.

I didn't ask for any of it—all I wanted was to belong. But instead of belonging, I spent much of my childhood on defense, trying to prove I deserved to be loved. Trying to justify my existence without guilt.

When my younger brothers were born, I faded even further into the background. The noise in the house got louder, but the space for me got smaller. It became painfully clear: I didn't fit. Not the way a child should feel they belong. There were nights I stared at the ceiling and wondered if I had been adopted. That's how out of place I felt in my own family—like a guest in a house where everyone else knew the rules but me.

Even as a little girl, I was a watcher. I saw everything. I listened not only to what was said, but—maybe more importantly—to what wasn't. I witnessed things no child should ever have to witness, and somewhere in my young mind, I thought: These people are crazy. And they were. Loud, unpredictable, messy—but mine.

I was born and raised in Washington, DC, right in the middle of it all. DC wasn't just monuments and marble buildings—it was rowhouses stacked tight, corner stores that knew your business, and neighbors who could hear your mama holler from two streets over. It was the sound of go-go music spilling out of car windows, the smell of fried fish and mambo sauce on Fridays, the hum of a city that never really went quiet. That was the backdrop of my childhood: gritty, alive, and unforgettable.

And then there was me—a Taurus, the bull—stubborn, determined, full of quiet strength and not-so-quiet opinions. That alone should tell you a lot about me. But trust me, there's more. I learned early that if you keep your mouth shut and your eyes wide open, you'll figure out everything you need to know. And if you're me, you'll file it away, roll your eyes when nobody's looking, and think: Lord, I really hit the jackpot with this family.

My parents separated when I was still little, not long after my first brother was born. Overnight, our house shifted. The energy felt different, the air heavier. I grew up in a single-parent household where survival was the focus and tenderness was a luxury.

Looking back, I realize I never had a clear picture of what a healthy relationship looked like. Children live what they learn, and when all you see are broken habits, you absorb them without realizing it. You memorize the rhythms of dysfunction as if they're normal. You mistake chaos for closeness. You inherit patterns you didn't ask for. And those patterns don't stay put—they travel. They pass down. One day that child becomes an adult, carrying trauma and pain they can't name or explain. That's exactly what happened to me.

I was a sad kid—not just sad, but haunted by questions no child should have to ask. Sad because I thought I was adopted. Sad because I felt like I didn't belong. That feeling became the lens through which I saw everything. I became afraid—afraid that if I wasn't perfect, I'd be sent away too. Afraid that love had conditions. Afraid that belonging could vanish overnight. So I performed, I hustled, I tried to be good enough for a place that already should have been mine.

At night, we would lay in bed with our heads hanging off the edge, staring at the ceiling upside down. She would talk for hours, her voice low and steady, pouring out story after story. I wouldn't say a word. I just listened. The stories were terrifying—children abandoned, abused, forgotten. And I believed every single one. I prayed silently that none of it would ever happen in real life.

Later, I found out they weren't just stories. They were her truth. Every horror she whispered in the dark was something she had lived. Pain was her bedtime story, and I was her audience. And when she died, the way she died was even worse than the stories she shared. It broke my heart in a way I didn't know a child's heart could break. It didn't just scare me—it confirmed what I already believed: the world could be an evil place, especially for little girls like us.

Even though I didn't know it at the time, those nights taught me how to carry other people's pain. I didn't yet understand my own, but I was already holding hers—tucking it into my small heart alongside my prayers, my fears, and my secret hopes. For years, I was terrified of having children. Not because I didn't want them, but because I was afraid of what could happen to them when I wasn't looking. Because in the world I knew, the people meant to protect you were too busy surviving to notice you were slipping away. But the predators? They never forgot. They were always watching.

The women in my family were loud, rowdy, and always into something. For the life of me, I couldn't understand why everything felt so chaotic. There was always yelling and fighting—not with strangers, but with each other. They were the most beautiful women I had ever seen. Always dressed to impress, flawless makeup, long hair that seemed to go on forever. But how could they be so beautiful, yet so ugly at the same time? Their attitudes poisoned everything, and the tension spilled into every room. And there I was, not fitting the mold. I didn't like long hair or makeup. I didn't want to be their mirror.

In sixth grade, I asked my sister to chop off my hair for graduation. She happily agreed—partly because my hair had grown longer than hers and she was eager to experiment. By the time she finished, the front was short and the back was long. A crooked little masterpiece. I just knew I was cute. But when my mother saw it, she spazzed out. She said she should shave my head bald for trying to be grown. I almost missed graduation because she was so furious. And yet, that haircut made me feel beautiful—it made me feel like me. To this day, I still don't like long hair.

I wet the bed for a very long time. My siblings called me nasty. Dirty. "Grown"—not because I was actually grown, but because in their eyes I was too old to still be wetting the bed. Their laughter echoed louder than my pain ever could. Nobody ever stopped to ask why.

I wet the bed because I was scared. Not just scared—terrified. Afraid to come out of my room at night. Afraid I'd get a beating if I even stepped out of bed without permission. Afraid of the dark. Afraid of the rats that ran through the house like they owned it. Afraid of what I might see—or what might see me.

Most nights I slept wrapped in my blanket like a cocoon, even in the summer heat. Sweat soaked my skin, but I stayed hidden because the fear of what might happen if I didn't was worse. I imagined rats crawling into bed with me, chewing on me, taking a piece of me in the night.

And then one night, one actually did. I had to pee so bad I couldn't hold it anymore. I pulled the covers down just enough to breathe and try to get up. That's when it bit me. Right on my chin. The pain was sharp, but the fear... the fear split my soul in two. I screamed so loud I thought the walls would crack. I peed everywhere—on myself, on the bed, on the floor. Tears mixed with the blood on my face as I ran to tell my mother. She didn't believe me. Told me I was making it up. Said I must've been dreaming. Sent me back to that same bed like nothing happened.

After that, I stopped saying anything. I stopped trying to explain myself. I just stayed silent. Stayed small. Stayed under those covers. And I wet the bed—night after night after night. Because it felt safer to be soaked in shame than to face what waited in the dark. It wasn't about laziness. It wasn't about not knowing better. It was about survival. And no one ever cared to ask.

But when I stayed with my grandmother, everything changed. The bedwetting stopped. The fear eased. The shame lifted. My body could finally exhale. She wouldn't beat me—even if I did wet the bed. She wouldn't scream. She wouldn't shame me. She would just quietly help me clean it up, whispering, "It's alright, baby," before tucking me back in and kissing my forehead. For the first time, I felt safe. Not because the world suddenly became less cruel, but because I had finally found a soft place to land.

She didn't ask questions I wasn't ready to answer. She didn't make fun of me. She just loved me as I was—fear and all.

Her house didn't have much, but it had peace. Her arms, her voice, the way she prayed in the morning, and hummed at night—all of it made me feel like I could breathe again. I don't think she ever knew what a gift that was to me. How just being with her helped me heal something that had been broken for a long time. She was the first person who made me feel like I was more than my mistakes. More than the mess I made. More than the shame I carried. And that safety—that sense of being seen without being judged. That's what finally set me free.

Now, when I see my niece or cousin struggle with the same thing, I see myself. I see that quiet shame in their eyes, the way they try to hide the truth—just like I did. And I don't laugh. I don't judge. I wonder what happened to them. What secret fear they're carrying. What they're too afraid or ashamed to say out loud. Because I remember. I remember what it felt like to live in silence. To soak the sheets and then soak in guilt. To wake up terrified of what would happen next.

I understand why they keep it to themselves. Getting beat for something you don't understand only adds more shame. And shame? It doesn't wash out easy. It stains everything. Your confidence. Your voice. Your worth. I stayed embarrassed for years until I finally realized the truth: It wasn't my fault. It was never about being nasty. It was about being scared. Alone. Unprotected.

Children don't just wet the bed for no reason. Sometimes, it's trauma showing up in the only way a child knows how to release it. Sometimes, it's the body crying out when the voice can't. Now, I choose tenderness. I wrap those babies in grace the way I wish someone had wrapped me. I tell them, "It's okay. You're okay." Because sometimes those are the words that begin the healing. And if I can be the safe place that stops the shame, then maybe that's the part of the cycle I was born to break.

Growing up, I was always marked as different. My oldest sister was short, dark-skinned like my mother, with long, pretty hair, a size 0 frame, and small feet. My middle sister was average height, fair-skinned, size 10, with medium-length hair, knocked knees, and an average foot size. And then there was me. Taller than my oldest sister but shorter than the middle, light brown-skinned, long hair, size 14, and shaped like my father's mother.

Somehow, the world decided that made me the "pretty one." Not smart, not kind, not funny—just "the pretty one." I never asked for the label, but it followed me everywhere. People would point it out like it was some badge I wore. I didn't think much of it at first, not until the moments when I wasn't there. Someone would ask, "Where's your sister?" and the reply would come: "Which one?" The answer was always the same—"The pretty one." That's when the shade would roll in. The cutting looks. The dismissive tone. Like I wasn't all that. Like being called "pretty" was a curse I didn't earn and didn't want.

It wasn't my fault how people saw me. I didn't control the comparisons, the labels, the way the world stacked us against each other. But somehow, I carried the guilt anyway—like being light-skinned, or shaped differently, or praised for something I never asked for was a crime I had to pay for. And the ones I paid to were my own sisters. All I wanted was to belong. To be seen for more than how I looked. To be loved without the asterisk of jealousy, without the weight of other people's opinions pressing between us.

There's no such thing as a perfect parent. No such thing as a perfect child. We all do the best we can with what we have. But sometimes, what we have isn't enough. Sometimes, we pass down pain we never meant to. Sometimes, we drop the ball—not because we wanted to fail,

but because we were never taught how to hold it in the first place.

In my case, both of my parents dropped the ball. They didn't just fumble it. They let it roll away, and I was the one left chasing it, all through childhood, trying to make sense of what I was missing.

My mother got a second chance. She's still here. She got to try again. She got to hear my truth, even when it hurt her. She got the opportunity to apologize, to show up differently, to rebuild. And whether it was perfect or not, we got something.

But my father... he gained his wings before he could ever make it right. Before I ever heard the words, "I'm sorry." Before I ever felt what it was like to be his daughter—not just a child he helped create. We got to air some things out before he passed. There were a few conversations, a few tears, a few cracks in the silence. But we never got to build the bond I always longed for. The kind of bond I imagined in my head so many nights growing up. A strong father who protected me, chose me, saw me. I never got that.

And I carry that with me.

There's grief in that kind of absence. Not just the grief of losing someone, but the grief of never having what you needed while they were still alive.

Sometimes I wonder...

Did he think about me as much as I thought about him?

Did he ever wish he had done more?

Did he ever cry over the time we lost?

I'll never know. And that's the part that still haunts me. That's the part that still hurts. The unfinished chapter. The empty seat. The silence that can't be filled.

I wish we had more time. I wish I had more memories. I wish I didn't have to write about a father wound instead of a father's love. But even in all that pain—I forgive him. Not because he asked. Not because he earned it. But because I need peace more than I need explanations.

And maybe that's what grace really is... Loving someone in spite of what they couldn't give.

REFLECTION

Fear became my first language. Before I even knew how to name it, it was teaching me lessons about silence, shame, and survival. These nights taught me how to shrink myself, how to bury pain under quiet obedience, how to stay small enough not to be noticed.

But they also taught me something else: the difference between fear and safety. My grandmother's gentle hands showed me that love doesn't humiliate—it heals. Her simple, steady kindness was the first glimpse I had of what safety could feel like. And even now, as a grown woman, I carry both truths inside me: the ache of being unseen, and the memory of finally being held without judgment.

CLOSING PRAYER

Dear God,

Thank You for keeping me—even when I didn't know I needed keeping.

Thank You for the fire You placed in me, the kind storms couldn't put out.

As I close this chapter, help me carry the lessons without the weight. Let me honor where I came from, but no longer be bound to it. Turn my scars into reminders of strength, and my pain into purpose.

Guide me forward—not just to survive, but to rise. To heal. To reclaim. To live fully and freely.

In Jesus' name,
Amen

THE FIRE IN ME

*T*his was the beginning of the war I was born to win.

I entered a world I never asked for—a world scarred by silence, shaped by struggle, and soaked in generational pain. I was molded by battles that began long before me, wounded by choices that weren't mine, and taught to survive storms I couldn't even name. I lived beneath shadows that tried to silence me—shadows I never cast.

But even then, something sacred was stirring inside me. God had already lit a fire in my soul that no dysfunction could smother—a purpose deeper than pain, a calling louder than chaos. The fire in me burned hotter than every storm sent to drown me.

I wasn't born to blend in with brokenness. I was born to break the cycle. I wasn't here just to survive the curse—I was chosen to destroy it.

This wasn't just about finding my place in the family. This was about claiming my purpose. They didn't see it. And for a long time, I didn't either.

But even in my unknowing, heaven knew exactly who I was becoming.

Chapter 2

SEARCHING FOR SAFE PLACES LONGING FOR LOVE

✦✦✦✦✦✦✦

"I wasn't just escaping the noise—I was slowly discovering the woman I was meant to become."

✦✦✦✦✦✦✦

I was born into the storm, but somehow, the fire inside me kept burning. As I got older, I began searching not just for survival, but for places where I could breathe. Places where I could laugh without fear. Places where I could be myself, even if I didn't fully know who that was yet.

In those years, life felt lighter. For a while, I found the safe places I had been craving for so long—in friendships, in young love, and the small victories of discovering who I was outside of my family's shadow. I became a cheerleader. I joined the swimming team. I started making my own friends, not just tagging along behind my sisters like I always had. For once, I wasn't just surviving—I was living. And it felt good.

My first boyfriend was a little older than me, and he treated me with a kindness and respect that felt brand new. He showed me what it was like to be seen to be valued.

It wasn't perfect, but it was pure in a way that mattered to a girl who had grown up always feeling invisible.

I didn't know it at the time, but two of the girls I laughed with after school, gossiped with late into the night, and dreamed big dreams with, would become my best friends for life.

One was my cousin. The other one was a girl from around the way. They weren't just friends. They were safe places, too. This was the beginning of something new. A new kind of hope. A new kind of fight—the quiet kind that says, I want more than the life I was born into. And for the first time, I truly believed that maybe, just maybe, I could find it.

Adolescence brought a lot of firsts—first boyfriend, my first taste of independence, and the first real friendships that shaped the woman I would become. There was something freeing about those moments. For the first time, I felt like I could carve my own path. I didn't want to follow the same patterns I had seen in my family. I wanted more for myself, and I began making small but powerful changes. It was the first time in my life that I felt like I was writing my own story, one step at a time. I wasn't following. I was leading—even if it was just leading myself. I was starting to figure out what made me happy. And honestly, for a while, life was sweet.

But happiness can sometimes stir up storms in other people, especially when they haven't found it for themselves. At first, I didn't notice the looks, the small jabs, or the way my siblings' jokes started to cut a little deeper. I was too busy living—cheering at games, practicing flips and kicks, swimming laps, laughing with my girls. But slowly, it crept in. The feeling that my happiness was a spotlight, and not everyone liked standing in its glow. I don't know if it was jealousy, resentment, or just old family habits—but somewhere along the way, I became a target again. Not because I had done anything wrong. Simply because I was shining.

Somehow my middle sister and I ended up on the same swimming team and all three of us was on the same cheerleading team. It was fun for me at first. I went along to get along. At first, I didn't want to believe it. I told myself I was imagining things—that maybe I was being too sensitive or reading too much into it. But deep down, I knew better. The little comments started first—small jabs disguised as jokes. Then the whispers, the jealousy, the cold stares.

I had fought so hard to feel like I belonged somewhere, and just as I was beginning to find my footing, I could feel the ground shifting under me again. Only this time, I wasn't that scared little girl anymore. I had a taste of something better—self—worth, freedom, happiness - and I wasn't about to let it slip away without a fight.

At first, it hurt. Then it confused me. Why couldn't they just be happy for me? But deep down, a stronger voice started rising inside of me—louder than the doubts, louder than the fear. A voice that said, "You don't have to dim your light to make other people comfortable."

I didn't know it yet, but that belief—that stubborn refusal to shrink—would become one of my greatest survival skills in life. For now, though, I was still learning. Still finding safe places. Still building the kind of life I had once only dared to dream about. Even though I was starting to carve out my own path, the reality of my home life was never far behind.

I lived in a house with my older sister and two younger brothers until my early adolescent years. My sister was always into something, and my brothers - well, boys will be boys.

It was always a madhouse, loud and chaotic, with my mother yelling about something or someone at any given time. The walls of our home were paper-thin, but the noise—the chaos—felt like it could shake the very foundation.

My sister was in junior high school by the time the boys started gravitating toward the streets. They found their own way—not always the right way—and most of the time, that left me home alone. I was the obedient one. The one who tried to do everything right. I didn't want the beatings my mother handed out like candy on Halloween. I was scared to death of her and so were most of my friends. So, I stayed in line majority of the time.

Growing up in that house, the safest place wasn't within the walls of home; it was outside of it. I spent as much time as I could in the fresh air, laughing, and living with my around-the-way friends. I stayed busy between the cheerleading team at the recreation center, the swim team, and hours spent at the neighborhood pool. I was gone all day, carefree and smiling, soaking up every second of freedom I could find. When I finally made it home, all I had time to do was eat and crawl into bed, grateful for the quiet moments before the next day's noise began again.

Outside, I found pockets of peace. Outside, I was just a girl—not the middle child, not the target, not the problem—just me. And maybe, just maybe, that was the first time I realized:

Home wasn't always a place. Sometimes, it was a feeling you had to find yourself. It was during those long, sun-drenched days that some of the most important people in my life found me.

My first real boyfriend, a little older, kind and patient, showed me what it felt like to be respected. It wasn't perfect. We were just kids, but he treated me like I mattered.

He saw me in a way that no one really had before. Around the same time, two of my closest friendships were born—bonds that would carry me through some of the hardest and happiest moments ahead.

My first cousin and a girl from around the way quickly became my safe spaces. We laughed together, dreamed together, and started to quietly build lives outside of the noise I was born into. Without even knowing it, I had started creating a family of my own choosing—one rooted in loyalty, love, and the freedom to simply be.

For the first time, I wasn't following behind my sisters or doing what everyone expected of me. I was carving out my own path, even if it started with small steps, choosing my own friends, and spending time with people who made me feel seen, not controlled. I didn't have the words for it then, but I was beginning to understand that my life could look different. That I could want different things. That I deserved different things.

Every laugh, every swim meet, every long summer night spent with my friends felt like I was stitching together pieces of a future that, deep down, I knew I wanted—even if I wasn't sure yet how to get there.

Somewhere between the laughter, the pool days, and the late-night talks with my best friends, I found small pockets of safety—safe places where I could breathe, dream, and just be. No expectations, no targets on my back, no heavy labels to wear. Just me—a girl learning how to enjoy life without looking over her shoulder.

My first boyfriend played a big part in that, too. It wasn't about big gestures or fancy gifts—it was the way he listened to me, the way he made me feel like my voice mattered. For the first time, I felt what it was like to be valued, not used or overlooked.

My best friends—the ones I met "around the way" and my cousin who became more like a sister—were the beginning of the family I chose for myself. We created our own little world where loyalty wasn't just a word you said—it was something you showed, day after day. These moments, as small and ordinary as they seemed back then, would later become the foundation for everything I would build up with, the roots of my strength, the beginnings of my fire.

Just when life started to feel like it was coming together, the cracks at home grew wider.

By the time I hit junior high school, my older sister was doing her own thing. She was busy living her life, wrapped in her own world, which meant that some of the chaos between us finally started to slow down. But peace in one corner meant war in another. That's when the problems with my middle sister started to escalate.

We clashed in ways that felt deeper, sharper. It wasn't just normal sibling rivalry—it was something heavier, something that constantly made me feel like I had to defend my space, my happiness, and even my right to exist peacefully. It was like I couldn't catch a real break.

Just when I found pieces of myself—through cheerleading, swimming, my friends, my first taste of young love—home would remind me that survival was still a daily battle. It wasn't fists flying, it was something worse: silent treatments, sneaky jabs, being blamed for things I didn't do. It was emotional warfare, and I was too young to even call it that. Still, I held on tightly to the life I was building outside those walls. Every cheer competition, every afternoon at the rec center, every late-night phone call with my best friends became little rebellions. Little declarations that I deserved happiness, no matter how much dysfunction tried to steal it from me.

My middle sister, who lived nearby, suddenly became a constant presence. Even though we didn't live together, it felt like she was everywhere I turned. We went to the same junior high school, and this was the period where she wanted everything I had—everything I was. If I joined a team, she wanted to join it, too. If I made new friends, she found her way into the circle. If I had a boyfriend, she made sure she was close to his friends. It drove me crazy, not because I didn't want to share my world, but because it felt like I could never have anything that was just mine.

I was fighting so hard to find my own identity, and somehow, she kept blurring the lines.

It was exhausting. Everywhere I went, I felt like I had a shadow, but not the kind that protected you—the kind that competed with you. Still, I refused to let it break me. I held onto my small wins: cheerleading practices, swim meets, long summer days at the neighborhood pool, laughing until my stomach hurt with my friends. Those moments were my escape. My proof that I could still carve out a space for myself, even when it felt like everyone wanted a piece of it.

Even though I was starting to carve out my own path, the reality of my home life was never far behind. Looking back, maybe that's when I first learned how important it was to protect my peace. Even when the world around me felt crowded, even when it seemed like I couldn't have anything just for myself, I started understanding that happiness wasn't something you stumbled across; it was something you had to fight for, piece by piece. And for the first time, I wasn't just surviving. I was starting to build a life of my own, one choice at a time.

Even when it felt like I couldn't have anything that was truly mine, I refused to stop moving forward. I didn't have all the answers, but I had a dream tucked deep inside—a dream of something better, something peaceful, something real. I was learning that my life didn't have to look like anyone else's. I could build something new, even if I had to build it from scratch.

I could fight for the life I deserved—one choice, one step, one prayer at a time. They could copy my steps, steal my shine, and try to rewrite my story, but they couldn't touch what was inside of me.

I was born with fire in my bones and a dream in my heart. And no matter what I faced, I would find a way to rise. I wasn't just surviving anymore. I was starting to live. Some days, it felt like my life wasn't mine at all—like I was just a shadow moving through the motions, carrying the weight of other people's choices, expectations, and pain. But deep down, beneath the noise, the chaos, and the heartbreak, there was a quiet voice that never stopped whispering,

"You are meant for more." That voice became my anchor. My lifeline.

Even when I was exhausted from pretending I was okay, even when fear wrapped itself around my dreams, I held on. I clung to that whisper when everything else told me to give up. Because something inside me refused to die. The girl they tried to break… survived. And one day, she stood up—bruised but not broken—and said, This story is mine now.

Not a continuation of anyone else's narrative.

Not a reflection of my past.

Mine.

And I was finally ready to write it.

In truth, in power, and on my own terms

CLOSING PRAYER

God,

I've spent so long searching for safety in all the wrong places. Teach me how to rest in You—where love is steady, and peace is real. Help me release the weight of needing others to validate me. I want to be whole. I want to be free. Wrap me in the safety of Your arms and remind me: I've always been loved.

In Jesus' name,
Amen

Chapter 3

UNSEEN WOUNDS

◇◇◇◇◇◇◇◇◇◇

*"For years, I called it strength. But now
I understand—it was survival.
And there's a difference."*

◇◇◇◇◇◇◇◇◇◇

I've been in two physically abusive relationships. And for the longest time, I convinced myself it was okay because I didn't just take the hits, I hit back. I told myself, "It's not abuse if I don't let them beat me." I wore my resistance like armor, thinking it made me strong. But the truth is—I was still bleeding beneath that armor.

I normalized the violence because I had grown up watching it. It felt familiar. And when pain feels like home, you stop realizing how deeply it's destroying you. A part of me always knew it wasn't right— that's why I never told anyone. I hid the bruises, masked the fear, laughed off the chaos. I never called it what it was.

But now, I say it without shame: I was in abusive relationships. And I survived them.

I don't know how I made it out without completely breaking down. There were days I thought I'd lose my mind. Nights I cried in silence, begging God to let me sleep through the pain.

One day, my therapist looked at me and said, "You were paralyzed by fear." And I finally had the courage to admit it, she was right. Fear had me frozen. Afraid to leave. Afraid to speak. Afraid that maybe no one else would love me. Afraid that this was the best I'd ever get.

But fear doesn't own me anymore. I broke out of the prison I was too scared to name. And now that I'm free, I see it everywhere—the signs, the patterns, the pain hidden behind fake smiles and tired eyes. I can spot it in a woman's silence. In her forced laughter. In the way she flinches when someone raises their voice.

That's the hardest part now—knowing what I know, feeling what I've felt, and seeing the unspoken cries in others. I used to feel powerless. Now I feel purpose. Because those unseen wounds? They taught me how to fight the right way. Not with fists. But with truth. With healing. With boundaries. With the understanding that survival was never the goal—freedom was.

Toxic people don't change—they change victims.

Emotional abandonment is one of the deepest wounds a person can carry. I know because I grew up with parents who never said I love you or wrapped me in their arms. They were emotionally detached— physically present but distant, almost unreachable. I didn't realize how much that absence shaped me until I became a parent myself.

I thought showing up and being a great provider made me a good mother. I paid the bills. I kept the lights on. I made sure my children had clothes on their backs and food in their stomachs. I told myself, "This is love." And it was—but only part of it.

When my children were born, I loved them with everything I had. I hugged them. I kissed them. I showed up for school events. I protected them fiercely. I gave them the best version of me I knew how to give.

But when it came to emotional intimacy—the softness, the stillness, the presence—I struggled.

I didn't know how to slow down. How to listen with my heart and not just my ears. How to hold their pain without trying to fix it. How to let them cry without feeling like I had failed. Because for so long, I had been told that survival was strength, and emotion was weakness. So I became strong. But I also became emotionally distant, and I didn't even realize it.

I thought I was doing enough. I thought love looked like sacrifice and struggle. But it wasn't until I got pregnant with my baby boy that something inside me unraveled.

That pregnancy cracked me open in ways I didn't expect. I cried all the time, and not just from hormones. I cried because something deep in me was waking up. I cried because old wounds were surfacing. I cried because I was finally feeling things I had spent my whole life burying.

I was grieving the childhood I never had while carrying the child I prayed for. I was angry. I was broken. I was exhausted. But most of all, I was aware. That baby boy forced me to sit with myself in a way I never had before. He didn't even have a voice yet, but somehow he was already teaching me how to feel. How to soften. How to be present, not just provide.

And that realization shattered me—because I saw all the times I thought I was "doing enough" and realized I had missed so many emotional moments that mattered.

But I also forgave myself. Because I didn't know what I didn't know. And now that I do, I'm learning how to love my children not just with action, but with connection. Not just with protection, but with presence. I'm becoming the mother I didn't have and the one my children deserve.

Unfortunately, I had to learn the importance of emotional connection the hard way. But that awakening, painful as it was, became the beginning of healing—not just for me, but for how I show up as a mother.

If I can reach just one person by sharing my story, that's enough for me. Because the truth is, people don't like to listen when they're still trapped. They're quick to say, "That could never be me," and in that very moment, they've already opened the door for it to be them. That kind of thinking blinds you to the red flags right in front of you. I still feel afraid sometimes, but the idea of allowing someone else to control my life again. That gives me the strength I need to keep going.

I'm always busy. My days are overloaded with tasks and responsibilities. I have yet to truly learn how to take a break when I need one. I always say I will—but I never do. Eventually, my body makes the decision for me. I crash. I shut down for days at a time. I've literally driven to South Carolina for an event, turned around and drove back the same day, and went straight to work. And I've done that twice in one week just to support someone I care about. I was exhausted, but I didn't regret it because the person I did it for loves and supports me on the same level.

I was my own problem. And that's the hardest truth I've ever had to swallow.

For years, I walked around with a bleeding heart, wondering why no one treated me the way I treated them. Why they didn't show up for me like I showed up for them. Why they didn't love me the way I loved—fully, completely, without hesitation.

Every time someone disappointed me, it felt like a personal betrayal. I gave people the best of me—and when they gave me crumbs in return, I internalized it. I started to question my worth. What's wrong with me? Why don't they care the way I care? One day, my husband looked at me and said something I'll never forget. He said, "Nobody will ever do what you do. You have to stop expecting people to be you."

And just like that, it hit me. I had been holding people to a standard they never agreed to meet. Expecting reciprocity from people who didn't even understand the language of the love I gave. I thought going the extra mile meant they would, too.

But they weren't me. And that realization both broke me and freed me. I started to really look at myself—at how much I give, how deeply I love, how hard I fight for the people I care about. And for the first time, I saw the full weight of what I bring into relationships. It's not a bad thing. It's just... a lot. I don't love halfway. I don't support with conditions. I don't know how to give less than everything.

But I finally understood: not everyone has the capacity to hold what I carry. And that doesn't make them bad—it just makes me different.

From that day forward, I stopped expecting people to match my energy. I stopped waiting for them to love like me, serve like me, show up like me. That's my gift. That's who I am. I go big. I love hard. I give fully. Not because I'm trying to earn love, but because that's the fire God put in me. And now, I've learned to protect that fire instead of burning myself out trying to keep others warm.

Before I met my husband, I didn't know how to be just a little bit mad. I didn't do "mild." My anger came like a storm—sudden, loud, and all-consuming. There was no warning, no slow build. One minute I was fine, the next, I was an erupting volcano.

One day he looked at me and asked, "Why do you have to blow up over everything?" And for the first time, I stopped to think about it. I had no real answer, just instinct. That was how I had always been.

When I was mad, I was really mad. When I was nice, I was really nice. There was no middle ground. No pause. No filter. Just intensity—always. He told me, "You can be the sweetest woman in the world or the meanest—there's never an in-between." And he wasn't wrong.

But over time, I evolved. I got tired of being controlled by emotions that left me exhausted. Tired of exploding and then picking up the pieces—mine and everyone else's. I started doing the work. Learning how to feel without breaking things. How to be upset without becoming unrecognizable.

I don't get angry the way I used to. Now, I simmer more than I explode. I breathe before I speak. I walk away when I need to. But I still get irritated—mostly when people think I'm stupid enough to believe their lies. Let's be honest, nine times out of ten, it's my kids trying it.

Here's what life has taught me and it took years of lessons to get here: The second you stop letting people walk all over you... The second you stop making excuses for disrespect... The second you say "No more"—everything changes.

Suddenly, you're not kind. You're "difficult." You're not strong. You're "mean." You're not protecting your peace. You're "selfish." You're not finally standing up for yourself. You're "crazy."

But I know better now. People who benefit from your silence will always call you loud when you start speaking up. And manipulators? They don't hate your attitude—they hate your boundaries.

I used to think setting boundaries made me cold. Now I know—boundaries don't make me bitter. They keep me whole.

People love to label you when you no longer fit into their comfort zone. These days, they call me "bougie" like it's an insult. Just because I want more than struggle... more than survival... more than scraping by. Yes, I want a decent apartment where the walls don't talk back through gunshots and sirens. I want a dependable car—not one that leaves me praying at every red light. I want clothes that make me feel beautiful, not just covered. I want a career that pays me what I'm worth—not pennies for my peace.

And I won't apologize for that. Just because I grew up in the ghetto doesn't mean I have to stay there. The streets may have raised me, but they won't bury me. I still live in the ghetto, but I promise you I'm not staying. I will make it out. Or I will die trying. That's not bougie. That's determination. That's vision. That's survival on purpose.

I don't chase dreams to impress people—I chase them because I refuse to live beneath the life God has for me. I've tasted struggle. I've choked on lack. Now I'm hungry for stability. For peace. For more. And if "more" looks like the finer things in life, then so be it. I like what I like. I want what I want. And I'm allowed to want more than barely enough.

People forget—I've been selfless my whole life. I've literally given the shirt off my back. Shared food I needed for myself. Showed up for people who wouldn't even answer the phone for me. And even with all that giving... all that loving... For some people, it still will never be enough. But I'm done breaking myself to fit their version of "humble." I'm done apologizing for having standards, for dreaming bigger, for refusing to settle.

Call me bougie. Call me selfish. Call me whatever makes you comfortable. But I know who I am—and I will not shrink to make anyone else feel tall.

They see the confidence. They see the goals. They see the woman with her head held high, chasing something better. What they don't see is everything I had to crawl through to get here. They don't see the nights I cried myself to sleep because the lights were off and the food was gone. They don't see the sacrifices—the jobs I worked while sick, the moments I gave my last so my kids wouldn't go without.

They don't know what it's like to feel stuck in a place that feels like a trap, but still force yourself to believe that something better exists. They don't know how exhausting it is to keep hope alive when everything around you is screaming give up.

This fight for "more" didn't come from pride—it came from pain. It came from promising my children they would never have to grow up the way I did. It came from looking in the mirror and refusing to let brokenness be my legacy.

So yes, I want better. Not just for the sake of comfort, but because I deserve to heal in peace. Because my children deserve to see what it looks like when a woman refuses to break under pressure. Because I know what it means to settle, and I've already done enough of that for a lifetime.

I don't owe anyone an explanation for the life I'm building. I'm not asking for permission anymore. I'm not dimming my light to make others feel better about staying in the dark. I know what I carry. I know the cost of becoming this version of me. And I won't apologize for finally wanting to live, not just survive. Because there is nothing bougie about healing. There is nothing selfish about choosing joy. And there is nothing crazy about believing you were made for more, even when you come from nothing.

This version of me? She was forged in fire. And she's not going back.

Behind the smiles and the moments of joy, there were deep, unseen wounds. The dysfunction I grew up with, the trauma I silently carried, shaped my worldview and how I approached life. I began to understand that the wounds weren't always physical, but emotional and psychological. The things I couldn't see—my fears, insecurities, and unresolved pain—affected me far more than I realized.

I was afraid of everything, half the things that I did was because I wanted everyone to like me, I was a people pleaser. I jumped on board with everything that everyone was doing. The only time that I could be myself is when I was home alone, home with my baby brother or when I was with my friends. I never had to be different around them.

I had learned to mask my hurt, but the damage was still there. I carried the weight of my past everywhere I went, even as I tried to forge a new path. My family's dysfunction had left scars on my soul, and these wounds would manifest in ways I didn't fully understand at the time. I began to grapple with the reality that some battles are fought within, often unseen by others, but deeply impactful.

As I got older, things started to change. The older I got, the more I felt out of place, like I didn't quite fit into the world that was expected of me. I paid more attention, noticing how everything seemed to clash with my inner desires. High school was the turning point. It was there that I started to come into my own. I no longer wanted to follow the crowd; I wanted to follow my heart, even if it meant stepping away from everything familiar.

I realized I didn't want to live in my family's shadow anymore. So, when most of my family and friends went to Dunbar High School, I made the decision to go to McKinley Tech. It wasn't just a school choice. It was my way of marking the beginning of my own path. I wanted more—more than the life they expected me to lead, more than the limits I had been placed under.

After high school, my desire for change continued to grow. I didn't want to stick around, so I left. I went to Job Corps to get away from home. Already holding my high school diploma, I pursued a trade in culinary arts, completing phase one of the program. But something inside me still told me that I wasn't done. The world felt bigger than what I could grasp, and I was determined to take a leap into it.

That one decision, walking away from the Army, changed the trajectory of my life. Not in the way I expected. Not with instant success or a neatly written plan. But in the quiet, grueling way life teaches you when it's time to grow up, for real. I had to figure things out on my own, with no uniform, no rank, no mission handed to me. Instead, I had bills that didn't care about my feelings.

I had jobs that drained me. I had days where I cried in the car just to pull myself together before walking into work. But looking back, that decision taught me more about myself than the Army ever could. It forced me to find my own voice—not the one they train you to repeat. It pushed me to build a life by instinct, not instruction. It taught me how to be my own protector, my own provider, my own motivator.

And most of all, it taught me how to trust my gut. That little voice that says, "This path isn't yours." "This fight isn't yours." I used to ignore that voice, thinking it was fear. Now I know it was wisdom.

That decision showed me that I don't have to prove my strength by walking into someone else's battlefield. I don't need medals or stripes to validate the wars I've survived. Because the real war was always at home—In my mind. In my past. In my bloodline. And I've been fighting that war my whole life.

So no, I didn't enlist. But I learned discipline in the school of hard knocks. I learned endurance through heartbreak. I learned resilience by rebuilding, again and again. That decision? It was the first time I really chose me. Not survival. Not escape. Me. My safety. My future. My sanity.

And choosing myself—even when it hurt—became the blueprint for everything that came after.

I didn't know it then, but that moment was my awakening. The beginning of becoming the woman I am now: Not government-issued. Not world-defined. But self-made, scarred, and unapologetically whole.

The unspoken battles of life—began to show. They were unseen, hidden beneath the surface. I was forging my own path, but the scars of my past kept reminding me of where I came from. And while I was moving forward, I still carried the weight of the things I hadn't fully dealt with.

Right after junior high, I entered high school, and everything began to shift. I met my first love, and he was nothing like my first boyfriend. This relationship was different. He wasn't my first high school crush or someone I could easily brush off. He was someone who captivated me in a way I didn't fully understand at the time. The twist? He was my older sister's son's father's best friend.

The dynamic was strange. My sister, who had been a somewhat distant figure in my life, started to be around more. She introduced me to a different side of the world—a world that was more complex, more mature, and more exciting. And in the midst of it, I found myself falling for someone who was close to my sister, someone who, in many ways, was part of her world, not mine.

This relationship pulled me in different directions. I was still trying to find my footing and navigate my own life, but I was also drawn into this world that felt like it was teetering between familiarity and chaos. With my sister's influence more present, I was beginning to see and experience a side of life I hadn't before—one that wasn't always safe or kind but was full of new experiences. My first love seemed to be a doorway into that world.

Looking back, it was a time of emotional growth, but also of emotional confusion. I didn't know how to handle these new feelings, and with everything I was juggling—high school, family dynamics, and now my first love—I started feeling like I was losing control of the pieces of my life.

As I navigated through those early years, I realized how deeply the absence of my father affected me. I didn't have a man in my life to set an example of how a man should treat a woman, to show me what love looked like when it was done right. Without that guidance, I found myself searching for validation, for love in all the wrong places. I resented my father for not being there when I needed him the most. It wasn't just the lack of presence—it was the emotional void that came with it. The things I didn't learn from him; I had to learn the hard way.

The pain from his absence ran deeper than I could ever express. It wasn't just that he wasn't there physically; it was the emotional scar he left behind. Without a father figure to show me my worth, I found myself questioning my value, wondering if I was deserving of respect and love. I looked for answers in relationships, trying to fill a hole that no one else could, trying to fill the emptiness left behind by a man who had the potential to shape my entire world.

But I didn't know how to ask for what I needed, how to recognize when I was settling for less than I deserved. I didn't know what boundaries were because no one had shown me how to set them. I was left to navigate relationships in the dark, hoping I could somehow figure it out as I went along.

In hindsight, I see now how much of what I went through could have been avoided if I had known better, if I had someone to teach me those lessons along the way. But without that fatherly guidance, I stumbled through relationships, sometimes finding fleeting happiness, but mostly getting hurt. Every time I was hurt, the resentment I felt for my father only grew stronger. It was a vicious cycle that I didn't know how to break. I wanted to be loved, but I didn't know how to receive love in a healthy way.

In relationships, I ended up repeating the cycle I had witnessed in my family, unknowingly passing down the same dysfunction. I didn't want to admit it to myself, but it was there. It was like I was bound by invisible chains, feeling the weight of everything I never got from my father and trying to fill that void in any way I could. As I look back, it's clear now that I was carrying wounds I couldn't see. At the time, I didn't even know they were there. I grew up in an environment where dysfunction was normal. It was what I knew, what I saw every day. My first love, as much as I wanted to believe it was different, was nothing more than a reflection of the unhealthy patterns I had seen before. The arguments, the manipulation, the control—it all felt like what I had grown up with, like it was supposed to be that way. And because I hadn't been shown a healthy example of love, I didn't know any better. I didn't know what it meant to be treated with kindness, to have respect in a relationship. I thought the pain was just part of love.

I carried the weight of that relationship with me for years, convinced that love had to come with hurt. I resented my father for his absence in my life, not just because he wasn't there, but because he didn't set an example of how a man was supposed to treat a woman. I had nothing to compare it to. I was left to navigate relationships on my own, figuring things out by trial and error, and the errors came with scars. Scars I didn't even realize were there until I started to grow older, to see things more clearly.

This wasn't the kind of love I wanted, but it was the only kind I knew. The emotional manipulation, the power struggles, the cycles of highs and lows—it all felt so familiar. In the back of my mind, I knew something wasn't right, but I didn't know how to fix it. I didn't know how to break free from the chains that had been passed down to me. So, I stayed, convinced that I wasn't worthy of anything better, that love was supposed to be hard and painful. The scars from that first love weren't just physical. They were deep in my heart, in my spirit. They were the kind of wounds that no one could see, but they shaped how I walked through the world.

What I didn't realize then was that my wounds didn't define me. I didn't have to carry them forever. But that would take time. It would take me to learn how to love myself first, to see my worth, to understand that I deserved so much more than the dysfunction I had been raised in. It would take me to break free from those unseen wounds, those wounds I didn't even know I had until they bled through.

The emotional toll of those years didn't just disappear after I left that relationship. I carried pieces of it with me, fragments that would come up in unexpected places. It wasn't just the first love that had hurt me; it was the cumulative weight of years of trying to make sense of an absent father, a volatile home environment, and trying to prove myself worthy of love. It's like I was constantly running in circles, unable to break free from the toxic cycle.

By the time I reached my early twenties, the realization hit me hard. I had spent so much time running away from the dysfunction in my family and the mistakes of my past, but I was still walking around carrying that same weight. It was as if I had been running but never really moved forward. The truth was, I hadn't confronted the pain. I hadn't allowed myself to sit with it, to process it. I was too busy masking it with distractions, trying to prove to the world that I was fine. But inside, I was far from fine.

I didn't know how to love myself properly. It wasn't something I had been taught. I had learned to pour love into others, to help everyone else before myself, but never to fill my own cup. I had never been shown how to make my own needs a priority. Instead, I wore the burden of everyone else's needs on my shoulders, often losing sight of my own. It wasn't just in my relationships—it was in my friendships, too. I was always giving, always there for others, but rarely did I get the same in return. I was giving from an empty well, and it started showing.

But it wasn't just about giving to others. It was about the void I felt within myself, the gap between who I was and who I wanted to be. That gap created tension. That tension made me angry, confused, and frustrated with myself. I had no answers to the questions that plagued me: Who am I? What do I want? What am I supposed to be doing with my life? I couldn't answer them, and it ate at me. It made me feel broken, lost, and unsure of who I could become.

When I finally admitted to myself that I needed help, that I couldn't fix it alone, it was a wake-up call. I realized that my wounds weren't just emotional, they were mental, too. My patterns of self-doubt, fear, and insecurity had built walls around me, and it had kept me from seeing the truth: I was worthy of love, happiness, and peace. For the longest time, I didn't believe that. I didn't believe that I deserved anything better than what I had been given.

The road ahead wasn't going to be easy. But the first step was acknowledging that the wounds were real, and that they were still affecting me. It wasn't about erasing the past—it was about learning to live with it, to heal from it, and to choose a new path forward.

This man, the one I thought I loved, had ruined me for all other men. The damage he caused wasn't just physical—it was emotional, psychological, and deeply embedded in my soul. He had shattered my perception of love and trust in a way that I couldn't even begin to comprehend at the time. I told myself that I would never give my heart to another man again. How could I? How could I trust anyone after what he had done to me?

I promised myself that I would never be faithful. In my mind, I was going to treat every man like he treated me. I would be cold, detached, and keep my heart guarded at all costs. If I couldn't have love the way I imagined it, then no one would get that kind of love from me. My heart became an impenetrable fortress, and I wore a mask of indifference to keep myself from feeling the pain any longer.

I had convinced myself that I was better off this way. It felt safer to push people away before they had a chance to hurt me. After all, if no one could get close enough to love me, then I couldn't be hurt again. My relationships were transactional—surface level, no depth. I wanted to avoid real intimacy at all costs. And yet, even as I did this, I knew deep down that I was only punishing myself. The walls I built around my heart were suffocating, and even though I told myself I was protecting it, I was only cutting myself off from the very thing I craved: real, genuine connection.

But it was hard. It was hard because a part of me still longed for the love I had once believed was possible. A part of me still wanted to trust. But the fear was stronger than my desire. The fear of being vulnerable again, of letting someone in only to have them betray me like he did, kept me from ever truly giving myself to another person.

I became numb to love, to the idea of trust, to the idea of ever feeling like I was worthy of it again. I felt like I had lost that part of me—the part that believed in true love. I told myself it was better this way, but deep down, I knew I was lying to myself. I had let the darkness of that relationship take control of me, and for years it dictated my life and my choices. It shaped the way I saw myself and the way I interacted with others. It was like I was walking through life with a broken compass, lost and unsure of where to turn.

I was terrible, yes. But I wasn't just terrible to others—I was terrible to myself. I didn't allow myself the grace to heal, to forgive, or to grow. I held onto that anger and bitterness, and in doing so, I chained myself to my past.

The journey toward healing would be long, and it would require me to confront the parts of myself I had buried for years. I would have to face the truth of what I had endured and acknowledge the damage it had done. Only then would I be able to start the process of forgiving not just him, but myself.

I was so damaged, so lost in the cycle of hurt, that I believed marriage could somehow be the answer. I thought that maybe, just maybe, if I gave my heart to someone else, they could love me past my pain. They could fix me, heal me, make me whole again. I clung to the hope that love could erase the scars that had shaped me, that it could somehow save me from myself.

But I was wrong.

I got married three times, each time thinking that this was it, that this would be the person who would finally show me what love truly was. But each time, I found myself repeating the same patterns, caught in the same pain, and trapped in the same wounds I thought I had healed. The scars I tried to hide and suppress reared their ugly head every single time. No matter how hard I tried to be the perfect wife, no matter how much love I gave, the bitterness, the fear, and the anger from my past bled into my relationships.

I couldn't escape it.

With each marriage, I thought it would be different, but it never was. I didn't know how to truly open up to someone in a healthy way and free myself from the chains of my past. I was still carrying the weight of those old wounds, and they were affecting everything I touched. I was still trying to fight my own battles, yet hoping that someone else could somehow take my pain away. But no one could do that for me. They couldn't love me through what I hadn't yet learned to love in myself. And when the relationships crumbled, I realized the hard truth: I had been looking for healing in places it couldn't be found

The breakdowns, the emotional walls, the fights, the fear—each time, I found myself in the same place: alone and hurting. I couldn't escape the damage I had carried for so long. It wasn't their fault. It was mine. I was still broken, still carrying all the baggage from the past that

I hadn't dealt with. I was repeating history without even realizing it. And each failed marriage only reinforced the belief that I wasn't worthy of the love I so desperately craved.

Scars You Can't See

These unseen wounds almost cost me my sanity.

My big sister and I fought—physically—twice as teenagers. Both times were fueled by misunderstandings, by her belief that I had disrespected her friends in some form or fashion. But what started as anger left behind more than bruises—it left lifelong scars.

The first time, she struck me hard enough to leave a permanent mark just above my lip—a scar I see every time I look in the mirror. But the second time, the damage ran deeper. That fight didn't leave a bruise; it left a scar on my heart. One that no one could see, but one I still feel in the quiet spaces of my soul. It was like every wound that had never been addressed finally showed its face. But what hurt the most wasn't the hit... it was who it came from.

She was my sister. My blood. And in that moment, it felt like love had left the room. Like all the history we shared had been erased by a single act of rage.

That fight left a scar—not just emotionally, but spiritually. Because it broke something in me I didn't know could break. It made me question if healing would ever be possible between us. It made me wonder if love could survive that kind of pain. And even after all of it, I was still after her heart. Still hoping for her love, still craving her approval. I forgave her—but not without struggle. That forgiveness came through tears, confusion, and a heart that didn't want to harden. I held on to the belief that maybe, just maybe, sisterhood could survive the pain.

In the end, all I had done was drag more people into the mess of my unresolved pain. I had built relationships on a foundation of brokenness and expectation, hoping that someone else would fix me when it was something only I could do.

I felt like a failure. I felt like I had lost every time. But little did I know, the road to healing wasn't about someone else loving me through it. It was about me loving myself enough to heal, to confront my past, and to finally take responsibility for the scars that had shaped my life.

A New Fire Within

Something shifted deep inside me. It wasn't loud. It wasn't dramatic. It was quiet—like a slow, steady flame refusing to be put out. For the first time in my life, I didn't want to just survive anymore. I wanted to live. I wanted to heal. I wanted to break free from everything that had been handed down to me in silence and pain.

I realized that if I didn't change the story, it would keep repeating itself—through my choices, through my children, through generations I hadn't even met yet. And I refused to be the link that kept the chains intact. I wanted more than broken promises and heavy hearts. I wanted a legacy of healing, of strength, of love that wasn't laced with pain. It wasn't about being perfect. It wasn't about pretending I wasn't scared. It was about being honest enough to say, "This hurt me. This broke me. But it will not define me."

The fire inside of me wasn't fueled by rage anymore. It was fueled by hope. By the belief that I could be the one to break the cycle. By the stubborn, unshakable decision that the pain would end with me.

Chapter 4 would be the hardest part of my journey yet—facing the unseen wounds, the ones buried so deep they shaped who I became without me even realizing it. But now, for the first time, I wasn't afraid to face them.

The healing had begun. And I wasn't turning back.

CLOSING PRAYER

God,

I've carried pain no one could see—hidden beneath smiles, silence, and strength. But You saw it all. Every unspoken bruise. Every buried tear. Every time I broke in secret. I no longer want to pretend I'm okay when I'm not. Teach me to bring even the invisible wounds to You. Heal what I've learned to hide. And remind me that being seen by You is enough.

In Jesus' name,
Amen

Chapter 4

INHERITED BATTLES

<><><><><><><><>

"Generational battles met divine interruption—
God called my name and said,
'The war ends now.' And in that moment, I was
fighting for every soul connected to me."

<><><><><><><><>

Growing up, we were always told, "What happens in this house stays in this house." All the physical, mental, and emotional abuse stayed behind closed doors. I knew it wasn't right, but we were sworn to secrecy. This is my story. My truth—not theirs, but mine. The saddest part? The dysfunction became so normalized that when I tried to speak up, I was labeled "too sensitive" or dismissed as a "drama queen."

Eventually, I stopped saying anything. I had to toughen up, be hard like them, if I wanted to survive in this family. I didn't like to fight, so I found excuses when it came time to stand up for myself. "My stomach hurts," I'd say. It became my go-to. Eventually, they started teasing me for it.

The mention of my mother's name terrified me. I still remember my first real fight. A group of girls in elementary school made it their mission to torment me every single day. On the playground, during recess, even after school—they followed me home like shadows I couldn't outrun. I didn't understand why I was their target. Turns out, the ringleader had a crush on a boy I hung out with. He was just my buddy. I wasn't even into boys back then. But they assumed I was his girlfriend, and that was all the reason they needed to bully me.

One afternoon, they followed me home again. But this time, my aunt was standing on the porch. One of the girls shoved me hard, right up the steps. I tried to act like it didn't happen, but my aunt saw everything. She said, "I know damn well you're not going to let her push you like that." I froze. Silent. Trembling. She knew I was scared. Then she said the words that sent a chill down my spine. "Okay. You don't want to fight? I'm going to call Lib." That was all I needed to hear. Lib was my mama. And if I didn't fight that girl, I knew I was going to suffer the consequences.

So, I fought like my life depended on it because it did. I slammed that girl to the ground and didn't stop swinging until someone pulled me off of her. I earned a stripe that day. My mama wasn't about to be beating nothing over here. (LOL)

But just when I thought it was over, the next day the girl came back—this time with reinforcements. She brought her cousin to fight my aunt. What she didn't know was that my sister was home. The girl said, "Yeah, I brought somebody to kick your butt." My sister looked her dead in the face and said, "Well, kick it then." And she did. Literally. Kicked my sister right in the butt. The fight was on. I was sure the girl thought that my sister was a wuss like me boy was she wrong.

Suddenly, the girl I fought the day before jumped on my sister's back. I stood there like a deer in headlights. Scared. Again. But in my head I heard the warning: if I don't help my sister, my mama is going to beat my butt. So, I jumped in.

We fought until we were both tired, swinging like our lives depended on it. When I finally caught my breath and looked around, the girl cousin was getting jumped by the rest of my family. At that point, it wasn't a fight; it was a family reunion with fists.

As I got older, my heart hardened. I didn't just learn to fight; I became good at it. My attitude matched my pain. I finally fit in. But deep inside, I was still that broken little girl.

Some battles are handed down long before we even realize we are fighting them. Without warning, we are drafted into wars that began generations before us—wars rooted in pain, silence, brokenness, and survival. I didn't know it at the time, but I was carrying wounds that didn't even start with me. The things I saw growing up, the dysfunction I was born into, the silent rules I lived by—they all shaped the battles I would one day have to face.

I spent so much of my early life reacting to the pain that had been passed down to me. It showed up in how I loved, how I trusted, how I handled anger and disappointment. I was fighting battles that I didn't start, but I still had to find a way to end.

By the time I realized the damage that had been done, I was knee-deep in my own mess, still trying to outrun the pain of my past. It took years for me to even recognize that not every struggle was mine to carry—that some of the war inside me was inherited. And the hardest part was understanding that healing wasn't just about fixing my own wounds; it was about breaking the chains that had held my family captive for generations.

We often feel bound by generational curses, walking paths laid before us without realizing that we have the power to break free. Society tells us that if our parents were a certain way, we will inevitably follow the same patterns. But that's not true. I made a conscious decision to end the cycle of generational curses in my life. I refused to continue the destructive path, choosing instead to create a better life for myself and my family. It hasn't been an easy road, but we are on the right path now, even though we are still a work in progress.

Looking back, I can see how family history, dysfunction, and baggage played a significant role in shaping who I became. My weakness? Family. I always put others before myself. I'd sacrifice my needs to help those around me, always stepping in when I saw a need. I thought it was just who I was—someone who had to help. I loved helping others. It made me happy. But over time, I allowed myself to be hardened by the people I tried to help. I was often manipulated into doing things I didn't understand or pushed to take on responsibilities I wasn't ready for. Slowly, this sweet, eager girl turned into someone with an attitude, someone who lashed out, not knowing how to cope with the emotions that were building inside me.

I didn't understand what was happening to me, and I didn't know how to deal with it. The years went by, and that unresolved anger and frustration became part of who I was. It wasn't until I nearly had a breakdown at work that I realized something had to change. I was fighting myself—fighting between who I had become and who I wanted to be. I didn't even know how to stop the battle inside of me. At that moment, my supervisor at work sat me down, listened to me, and referred me to a therapist. At first, I resisted. I had grown up believing that therapy was something "other people" did. I told myself it wasn't for me. But months later, after another breakdown, I finally realized I couldn't keep pushing through. I had to face the internal struggle affecting every part of my life, including my work.

My employer gave me an ultimatum: get help or find another job. They didn't care about my personal issues—only that my work performance didn't suffer. Loving my job, I scheduled an appointment with a therapist. The day I walked through that therapist's door was the moment my life began to change. I didn't realize how much help I needed until I took that first step. I began therapy with the goal of finding balance between my work and personal life, but over six months,

I learned so much more. I learned to manage the challenges I faced at work and at home without letting them consume me.

But even after those six months, there was still more to uncover. The journey wasn't over. I still had so much work to do, but I was starting to heal. And for the first time, I could breathe, knowing that I didn't have to keep fighting alone.

The more I tried to move forward, the more my past kept pulling me back. Every relationship, every decision, every heartbreak was tied to something deeper—something I didn't know how to name yet. I was living out patterns that had been set in motion long before me, trapped in cycles of pain and broken trust.

As much as I wanted to be different, I realized that I couldn't outrun what I had never truly faced. I had to look back before I could move forward. I had to uncover the hidden wounds, the silent teachings, and the inherited battles that shaped the woman I had become.

And so, the real work began.

I grew up believing that survival was enough. If you could make it through the day without breaking, that was considered strength. Vulnerability was weakness, and emotions were to be swallowed, not spoken. The dysfunction I witnessed in my family wasn't something we talked about; it was something we lived. Anger, betrayal, abandonment—these weren't just isolated moments. They were patterns passed down like family heirlooms. The pain I carried didn't start with me. I had simply inherited it.

My father's absence left an aching void that I spent most of my life trying to fill. Without his presence, there was no blueprint for what real love was supposed to look like. No one to show me how a man should cherish and protect a woman. No one to tell me that I was worth being chosen, respected, and fought for.

Instead, I learned through experience—brutal, painful experiences. And every wrong relationship, every shattered dream, every time I stayed longer than I should have, I was living out that silent lesson:

you are not enough to stay for. By the time I realized how deep the scars ran, I had already survived too much. I had already been married and divorced three times, each marriage a desperate hope that maybe, just maybe, someone could love me enough to heal the broken places inside of me. But love can't fix what you won't confront. And the scars, no matter how much I tried to hide them, reared their ugly head every time.

I wasn't a victim anymore. I wasn't a little girl waiting for someone to rescue me. I had become a woman hardened by disappointment, armed with trust issues and an unshakable belief that if I didn't protect myself, no one else would. I became reckless with hearts—including my own—because deep down, I believed love was nothing more than a battlefield.

I spent years warring with myself, trying to reconcile the woman I wanted to be with the woman I had been forced to become. It took everything in me to admit that the battles I fought weren't just mine. They were battles passed down from generations before me—silent struggles, unspoken griefs, cycles no one ever dared to name.

But I was determined. Determined to be the one who would name them. Determined to be the one who would break them. The pain I inherited might not have been my fault. But the healing? That was going to be my responsibility.

There are words that stick to your soul, even when you try to shake them off. I remember one day, riding in the car with my daughter's father. Out of nowhere, he said to me, "You made a career out of being unhappy." He said it so casually, like he was talking about the weather. He had no idea.

I wasn't unhappy because of him. I was broken—shattered in places so deep that even I couldn't find all the pieces, buried beneath years of pain I never gave myself permission to feel.

I didn't realize then that these lessons were stitched into my DNA long before I ever had a choice.

Breaking The Silence

Healing didn't happen overnight. It didn't come wrapped in some grand moment of clarity or a perfect apology I had been waiting to hear my whole life. It came in whispers. In quiet decisions to choose myself, even when it hurt.

The first step was admitting that I was broken. Not because I was weak, but because I had been strong for too long. I had survived things that should have destroyed me, but survival wasn't living—it was just existing.

I started realizing the silence that surrounded our family—the unspoken wounds, the hidden pain—had been killing us for generations. Nobody ever named it. Nobody ever dared to say, "We are hurting. We need help." We just smiled through it. Laughed through it. Prayed through it. But healing requires honesty. And I decided that if no one else would break the silence, I would.

At first, the changes were small. Setting boundaries with people I once would have let walk all over me. Saying no without explaining myself. Allowing myself to cry without feeling ashamed.

I had to unlearn so much—like believing that love was supposed to hurt, or that loyalty meant staying in places where I was being broken. I had to teach myself a new language of love—one that started with loving myself first. It was messy. It was painful. But it was necessary.

I wasn't just fighting for myself anymore. I was fighting for every generation that had come before me and every generation that would come after. The cycle of silent suffering had to end with me.

And little by little, it did.

Learning A New Kind Of Love

Real love—the kind that builds instead of breaks—didn't come rushing into my life like some fairy tale. It came quietly, almost like a whisper. At first, I didn't recognize it. How could I? I had only ever known love wrapped in pain, promises followed by betrayal, hands that hurt more than they held.

I didn't know that love could be patient. I didn't know that love didn't have to make you choose between being yourself and being accepted. I didn't know that love could see the ugliest parts of you and still stay. So, when real love tried to enter my life, I almost rejected it. Pushed it away because it felt unfamiliar. Uncomfortable. Unsafe even, because safety was foreign to me.

I had built walls so high around my heart that even the good things had a hard time getting through. Walls made of distrust, bitterness, survival. I was guarded, skeptical, always waiting for the other shoe to drop. Because in my mind, it always did.

It took time—and a lot of patience—for me to even start believing that I deserved something different. Something better. Something that didn't hurt. I had to learn that love wasn't supposed to be a battlefield. It wasn't supposed to leave bruises on your soul. It wasn't supposed to make you question your worth.

Real love didn't demand that I lose myself to be loved. Real love didn't punish me for my past or weaponize my wounds. Real love stood there, steady, even when I flinched.

Slowly, I started to lower my defenses. Not because someone forced me to, but because I realized I wanted more for myself. I was tired of surviving. I was ready to live.

Steps Toward Healing

Healing didn't happen all at once. It wasn't a single decision or a perfect moment where everything suddenly made sense. It was messy. It was painful. It was waking up every day and deciding—sometimes through tears—I was worth fighting for.

The first step was admitting I was broken. Not flawed beyond repair. Not unworthy. Just broken—carrying wounds that needed tending, not hiding. I stopped pretending to be strong when I was hurting. I stopped shrinking myself to make others comfortable. I stopped apologizing for needing time, space, and grace to heal.

I learned how to set boundaries—real ones—not the invisible lines I used to draw that people crossed without consequences. I learned to say no without feeling guilty. I learned that protecting my peace wasn't selfish; it was necessary.

For the first time, I made myself a priority. Not to be cold. Not to be hard. But because I finally understood I couldn't pour from an empty cup. I couldn't keep giving parts of myself away and expecting to feel whole.

I started speaking up. I started praying differently—not just asking God to fix things but asking Him to heal me from the inside out. I journaled. I cried. I forgave people who never said sorry. I forgave myself, too—for staying too long, for settling, for surviving the only way I knew how.

Healing wasn't about becoming someone new. It was about remembering who I was before the world tried to break me. It was about reclaiming the pieces of myself that I had buried under pain, anger, and shame. It was about choosing to believe—even on the hardest days—my story wasn't over yet.

There are battles you fight in your own life, and then there are battles that are passed down to you. My story is not just mine—it's a continuation of a long, silent war. A war fought in the quiet corners of family history, carried through the years like an invisible weight.

I've spent so much of my life fighting to make sense of my pain, trying to untangle the mess of confusion, disappointment, and rage that has been handed down from generation to generation. It wasn't just me; it was my mother, my grandmother, and even those before them. Their pain, their brokenness, their survival instincts—I had inherited it all without even knowing.

I didn't ask for this fight, but here I was, standing in the middle of a battlefield I never knew existed until it was too late to turn back. How could I? How could I see that the wounds in my heart were part of a much bigger story, one that stretched far beyond the broken relationships and failed dreams I thought were only my own?

I spent years blaming myself for not being able to overcome the things that held me back. I thought if I just tried harder, loved better, worked more, that somehow I would fix what had been broken for so long.

But the truth is—I wasn't just fighting my own demons. I was fighting demons that were older than me. Demons that lived in the very blood running through my veins. I didn't have the luxury of being born into a world where love was shown in healthy ways. Where people knew how to communicate without violence or silence. Where emotional needs were met instead of buried. Where fathers stayed, where mothers healed, and where families were whole.

No, I was born into a war zone, and the weapons of that war were words left unspoken, love never given, and pain that couldn't be healed. My father's absence was the first battle I had to fight. But it wasn't just his absence—it was the fallout from generations of men who didn't know how to be fathers. How to be husbands. How to be present.

I've learned through pain and experience that it's not just the visible scars that leave their mark—it's the unseen ones. The things we inherit without ever realizing they're there. The belief systems, the unhealthy patterns, the coping mechanisms that have been passed down from mother to daughter, from father to son, like some invisible chain that tightens with every generation.

And I'm not talking about the obvious things—the physical abuse, the broken homes, the addiction. I'm talking about the more insidious things. The emotional neglect. The perfectionism. The silent expectations. The belief love should hurt or your worth is measured by how much you can endure.

When I was younger, I couldn't see it. I couldn't understand why I was always drawn to the same types of relationships—toxic, painful, always leaving me with more scars than I had when I entered them. But now, I see it clearly. I was following the pattern. A pattern that had been set long before I was born.

My family didn't know how to break free from it. They were stuck, and I was stuck with them.

I used to believe if I could just find the right person, if I could just be loved the right way, everything would change. But I came to realize the first person I needed to love the right way was me. I needed to learn to break the pattern—not just for me, but for my children, for my future.

It wasn't going to be easy. Breaking generational cycles never is. It meant facing the truth about my own wounds—acknowledging they were deep, they were real, and they weren't going to disappear just because I ignored them. It meant coming to terms with the fact I couldn't change the past, but I had the power to rewrite the future.

The real battle was not about fighting the people who had hurt me. The real battle was fighting to break free from everything passed down to me. And for the first time in my life, I was ready to do the hard work. I was ready to be the one to change the narrative. To rewrite the story that had been handed to me, one painful chapter at a time.

I couldn't undo the damage that had been done, but I could ensure my children would not carry the same burden I had. That they would grow up knowing love doesn't have to hurt. That they were worthy of respect, care, and tenderness. That their hearts weren't meant to be broken but cherished.

The inheritance I wanted to pass down to them wasn't pain. It was freedom. Freedom to love without fear. Freedom to trust without hesitation. Freedom to heal. But to give them that, I had to first heal myself. And so began the hardest battle of all: The battle to confront my past and finally break free from the cycles that had held me captive for so long.

This was the beginning of the fight for my freedom. A fight I was finally ready to win.

It's one thing to understand the weight of your inherited battles, but it's another thing entirely to confront them head-on. For most of my life, I believed survival was enough. I was surviving, but I was never really living. I was just going through the motions, moving from one heartache to the next, never realizing I was repeating the same mistakes over and over. Each mistake was like another chain in the shackles that kept me locked in the same cycle.

I thought being strong meant holding everything in—never letting anyone see the cracks in my armor. But what I came to realize was that my armor was suffocating me. I didn't need to be strong anymore. I needed to be whole. But how could I be whole when everything around me had taught me that being broken was normal? How could I break free from something that had been ingrained in me for as long as I could remember?

It took years of reflection, of peeling back the layers of pain and regret, to realize the greatest battle I was facing was not with others, but with myself. I had to confront the beliefs that had been handed down to me—beliefs I had carried with me without question, without even knowing they were there.

One of the hardest realizations was I had been living in a place of deep self-doubt. I didn't believe I deserved better. I didn't believe I was worthy of peace, of love, or of happiness. Every time something good came into my life, I sabotaged it. Every time I was on the brink of happiness, I'd find a way to destroy it.

I had convinced myself pain was the price I had to pay for love, that I wasn't meant to have something better. And the worst part? I had passed this belief on to my children without even realizing it. I had taught them, through my actions, love was supposed to hurt. That relationships were supposed to be hard.

I couldn't do that anymore. I couldn't live in that lie, nor could I allow it to be the inheritance I left for the next generation. I was tired of fighting everyone else for my happiness. It was time to fight for my own peace. That fight wasn't going to be easy. Healing never is.

There were days when the weight of it all felt unbearable. The weight of all the things I had carried, the things I hadn't even known I was carrying. It felt like I was dragging around a lifetime's worth of pain—and every time I thought I had let go of it, I found another layer of hurt I hadn't even known existed. But what I came to understand is healing doesn't happen overnight. It's a process. It's messy, it's uncomfortable, and sometimes it feels like two steps forward, ten steps back. But I was determined to keep moving forward, even when it felt impossible.

I started small. It was hard, but I began to change my mindset. I told myself I deserved peace. I told myself I deserved love. And I told myself that breaking the cycle of pain was possible—that I didn't have to live in the shadow of the generations before me.

I started setting boundaries—something I had never been able to do before. I began to say no when I needed to, to walk away from things and people that no longer served my peace. It felt unnatural at first. It felt wrong. But it was exactly what I needed to do in order to protect my heart, to protect my future.

The next step was forgiveness—not just of others, but of myself. That was the hardest part. For years, I had blamed myself for everything. For every failed relationship, for every mistake, for every heartache. I had told myself that I was unworthy, that I was broken beyond repair. But I couldn't keep living in that shame.

Forgiveness didn't mean excusing the hurt. It meant letting go of the anger and resentment that had been consuming me. It meant freeing myself from the grip of the past. And as I started to forgive, something beautiful happened. I started healing.

The healing was slow, but it was real. It wasn't about erasing the past; it was about learning to live with it. It was about making peace with the fact that I wasn't perfect, that I had made mistakes, but those mistakes didn't define me. They were just pieces of my story—pieces I had the power to change. I began to find joy in the small moments. In the love of my children. In the simple acts of self-care. In the quiet moments of reflection.

I stopped searching for validation outside of myself. I realized that I didn't need anyone else's approval to know I was worthy. I had to be the one to believe in my own worth. And through it all, I started to understand that breaking the cycle wasn't just about me. It was about all of us. It was about my children, my family, my legacy. I was breaking the chains, not just for myself, but for the generations to come. I was choosing to rewrite my story, to give my children a future free from the burdens of the past.

The fight wasn't over. It would never be over. But I was no longer fighting alone. And for the first time in my life, I believed I was worthy of peace. Worthy of love. Worthy of freedom. And I would never stop fighting for it.

As I reflect on the darkness of those years, I realize just how deeply I had been scarred. But I also recognize that it was in those very struggles my strength was forged. I didn't know it at the time, but every battle I fought, every broken piece of myself, was a part of the process of finding my way back to me.

I had to get to the point where I could stand face-to-face with my own reflection and say, "I'm enough." It wasn't easy. It took years of self-doubt, heartache, and mistakes. But eventually, I started understanding healing wasn't about erasing the past. It was about understanding it, accepting it, and choosing to break the chains that had held me captive for so long.

I had carried the weight of every disappointment, every betrayal, every loss, but I realized I didn't have to carry it forever. My history didn't define me; it simply explained who I had been. The person I was becoming had the power to rewrite the narrative. It wasn't easy to let go of the pain, but I had to. I had to do it for myself, for my children, for my future.

The road to healing was never a straight path. It twisted, turned, and sometimes even seemed to go backward. But each step forward, no matter how small, was a victory. And with every victory, I reclaimed a part of myself that I thought I had lost forever.

My past would always be a part of me. But it no longer had control over who I was becoming. I could look at my scars and see not just the pain but the strength that had come from enduring it. I wasn't broken anymore. I was rebuilding—stronger, wiser, and ready to step into a future where I no longer defined myself by the things I had survived, but by the woman I was choosing to become.

God. He saw past the armor I built to survive. He knew the real me—the one buried beneath the pain, the silence, and the survival mode. And slowly, He began peeling back the layers. Not to hurt me... but to heal me.

I used to think being broken meant being weak. Now I know—brokenness was the beginning of my breakthrough. God allowed me to be broken so I could walk in my purpose, not my pain.

CLOSING PRAYER

God,

I surrender the pain I've kept hidden for too long. I release the secrets that were never mine to carry. Help me see my brokenness through Your eyes—not as shame, but as soil for growth. Teach me how to heal out loud, walk in truth, and live in freedom.

In Jesus' name,
Amen

Chapter 5

MY OWN CROSSROADS

∞∞∞∞∞∞∞∞

*"Every crossroads forces a choice: repeat
the lesson or rise from it."*

∞∞∞∞∞∞∞∞

Ilived my best life when I was in high school. The teachers and students loved me—well, most of them did. I was on the cheerleading team, which made me a bit popular. I was a sophomore hanging with the seniors, and you had to be cool to pull that off. Participating in extracurricular activities was the highlight of my day during the week; that meant I didn't have to go straight home after school. My grandmother's house was always full of people. We only had one bathroom, one house phone with a single line, and no privacy. My grandmother was old school. She didn't want anyone interrupting her conversation when she was on the phone, and her line stayed busy. Can you imagine waiting to use the phone when one of your knucklehead brothers was on it?

As soon as you are on a positive track in your life, here come all of the negative obstacles that you expect to show up. For a brief moment, you second-guess everything you've worked toward. You say to yourself, "I can't do this. Maybe now isn't the right time to start that new adventure." Just for a moment you forget about all the blood, sweat, and tears you poured into yourself—the time and money you invested.

For a brief moment, I allowed doubt to set in. I wanted so desperately to give up, I almost gave up. But something unexpected happened that made me decide to keep pushing. No matter how slow the process, I will not give up or give in to my fear. I was afraid from the very beginning. Here I sit declaring to keep pushing. I started this journey for a reason; I'm determined to finish this journey for the same reason. I will try harder to get to my happy place. I have a lot of obstacles in my way, allowing myself to compromise who I am, who I aspire to be. I have to find the balance I need in order to succeed.

I believe everyone has that aha moment—that split second of clarity when your spirit finally says, "Enough is enough." It doesn't matter when your moment comes—what matters is that you honor it. Acknowledge it. Feel it. Then do what you need to do for you, unapologetically. That time for me is now.

Life threw some unforeseen situations my way—distractions, setbacks, detours I didn't see coming. For a moment, I lost focus. But the moment passed, and now I'm back on my grind, sharper than before. Fear tried to paralyze me, tried to convince me that I'd fail before I even started. But then I looked back at every storm I walked through, every obstacle I climbed, every "I can't do this" I survived.

And I realized—I never quit. Not once. I bent, but I never broke. And fear? Fear only wins if I stop moving. And that's not who I am. The race is not given to the swift nor the strong, but to the one who can endure to the end. And I was built to endure.

You know what I've never had? The luxury of just being me. No titles. No roles. No expectations. Just me. I've never lived alone—not once. I've always lived on autopilot, going through the motions, doing what needed to be done for everybody else. I never stopped to ask: *What do I want? What makes me happy? Who am I, really?*

I don't know who I am without being a mother, a wife, a girlfriend, a sister, an aunt, a friend. Those identities shaped me, held me together, gave me purpose. But now, I'm starting to wonder… Who would I be if none of those titles existed?

If there were no one left to pour into, would I even know how to pour into myself? Would I look in the mirror and recognize the woman staring back at me? Or would I only see the fragments—the many shadows of the person I became just to survive?

What I do know is this: I love the woman I've become in the last two years. She's not perfect, but she's real. She's healed in places that used to be raw and aching. She speaks up now. She sets boundaries. She chooses peace. Before that? I was living. But I wasn't alive.

Now I'm finally learning how to choose myself—not out of selfishness, but out of necessity. Because this version of me? She's not built on brokenness anymore. She's built on truth. And she's just getting started.

I was breathing for everyone but myself. Holding my breath for people who wouldn't even notice if I suffocated. Pouring from a cup that no one ever thought to refill. I gave everything—my time, my heart, my strength, my sanity. Always showing up. Always overextending. Always carrying the weight of everyone else's world, while silently watching my own dreams fade into the background.

I thought that being everything for everyone would make me enough. That sacrificing myself was proof of my love. That maybe—just maybe—if I gave more, they would finally see me. Value me. Choose me. But the truth is, I could give the best of me every single day and still never be enough for some people. Not because I lack anything—but because some people only know how to take.

So today, I stop waiting to be seen. I stop measuring my worth by their blindness. I stop holding my breath. I declare: I am enough for me. Enough in my silence. Enough in my softness. Enough in my strength.

Enough in my healing. I may not be everything to everyone, but I am everything to me. And from now on, I breathe for her.

Life has a funny way of forcing you to face yourself, especially when you spend years running from the very things that broke you. For a long time, I believed that changing my environment would fix my problems—new address, new job, new phone number, new people. But no matter how many fresh starts I chased, the same old wounds kept showing up, just in different places, wearing different faces.

I carried my pain from relationship to relationship, packing my unresolved emotions like luggage I refused to open. Instead of dealing with the hurt, I buried it. Instead of healing, I masked it. I thought if I could just move on fast enough, I wouldn't have to feel the weight of disappointment, betrayal, or abandonment. But the truth is, you can only outrun yourself for so long.

Love Without A Manual

I was married four times—twice to the same man. Make that make sense.

Even now, it sounds unbelievable when I say it out loud, but it was my truth. The kind of truth that most people would hide behind shame. But I promised myself I wouldn't do that anymore. This chapter isn't about judgment—it's about honesty, and I owe myself that much.

The truth is, I had no idea how to be a wife. I didn't grow up watching a healthy marriage play out in front of me. There was no blueprint, no quiet moments of love and partnership to mirror. I only saw survival. So, when someone asked me to marry them, I said yes, not because I was sure, not because I was ready, but because I thought being chosen meant I was worthy. And I desperately needed to feel worthy.

But saying "yes" doesn't mean you're equipped. And I wasn't. I entered marriage carrying wounds I hadn't named yet. I brought broken expectations, unspoken fears, and generational dysfunction that I hadn't learned to recognize, much less heal. I poured all of it into someone else, hoping love could hold it together. But love without healing isn't sustainable—it's heavy. And my love was heavy.

I didn't know how to be a partner because I was still trying to figure out how to be whole. I wanted connection, but I feared vulnerability. I wanted intimacy, but I didn't trust closeness. I wanted stability, but I had no foundation. The truth is, I wasn't looking for a husband—I was looking for a savior. And no man, no matter how good his intentions, could save me from wounds I hadn't faced myself.

Twice, I went back to the same man, hoping the second time would make up for everything we both got wrong the first time. But broken people breaking up and coming back together still doesn't equal healing. It was love, yes, but it was love tangled in pain, guilt, and unmet needs.

Still, I don't regret those marriages. They were part of my journey—mirrors that showed me what I needed to confront. Without them, I wouldn't have seen just how deep the patterns went. I wouldn't have known how far I still had to go.

So no, I wasn't ready. But I was willing. And from that place—as messy and complicated as it was—I learned what real healing demands: honesty, accountability, and the courage to stop blaming others for what I hadn't yet given myself.

I now know what I didn't know then—that love is not a rescue mission. It's a partnership. And before I could truly be one half of anything, I had to become whole on my own.

That realization didn't come overnight. It came in pieces—in therapy sessions, in tearful prayers, in lonely nights where I finally faced myself. I stopped looking for someone to complete me and started learning how to complete myself. I dug deep into the roots of my patterns, the unspoken lessons I had absorbed as a child, the lies I believed about my worth. And from that work, I began to rebuild.

Slowly, I learned to love without losing myself. I learned that a healthy marriage starts with a healed heart. And when I finally said "yes" again—truly and fully—it wasn't because I needed to be saved. It was because I had finally figured out who I was and what love was meant to be.

Eventually, everything I tried to suppress exploded all at once. The little girl inside me—the one who had felt invisible, unsupported, and unloved—demanded to be heard. The woman I had become—hardened by survival, silenced by shame, and exhausted from pretending—could no longer carry the weight.

Standing at the crossroads of who I had been and who I desperately wanted to become, I realized I had a choice to make: continue running from my pain... or finally stop, turn around, and face it head-on.

Healing was not an easy decision. It was messy, painful, and isolating at times. But deep down, I knew I couldn't keep living trapped by my own suppressed suffering.

I deserved better.

And for the first time in my life, I decided I was worth fighting for.

At first, healing didn't feel powerful. It felt terrifying.

For so long, survival had been my shield. Numbness had been my protection. Letting myself feel again—really feel—made me feel naked, exposed, and weak. But deep down, something kept whispering, "There's more to life than just surviving."

I didn't have a grand plan or a five-step program. I just started by telling myself the truth. I admitted that I was hurting. I admitted that I was carrying pain that didn't even start with me. I admitted that jumping from relationship to relationship wasn't healing me—it was destroying me even more.

I started by owning my story, even the parts I hated. Some days that looked like crying alone in my car. Other days it meant apologizing to people I had hurt along the way. It meant forgiving people who never apologized. It meant forgiving myself for all the reckless choices I made when I didn't know better.

It wasn't pretty. It wasn't quick. And it definitely wasn't easy.

But with every painful step, I was peeling back the layers of generational dysfunction, old betrayals, and buried disappointments. Layer by layer, scar by scar, I was reclaiming me.

For the first time in my life, I started seeing glimpses of the woman I was always meant to be. Not the scared little girl trying to survive. Not the broken woman trying to outrun her past. But a woman who knew her worth––even if she was still learning how to walk in it.

At first, the breakthroughs were small. Choosing to stay instead of running when life got hard. Speaking up for myself instead of swallowing my pain. Letting go of people who only loved me when it was convenient for them. Trusting my intuition, even when it didn't make sense to anyone else.

I realized healing wasn't about forgetting everything that had happened to me. It was about learning how to carry my story differently—without shame, without bitterness, without self-hatred.

The more I grew, the more I understood that brokenness and beauty could exist in the same person. That just because I had fallen before didn't mean I was doomed to keep falling. That I could choose better.

That I deserved better. And slowly, step by step, I did.

I learned how to love myself. Not the perfect version of me—but the real me. The me who had survived hell and still dared to hope for heaven. The me who could finally look in the mirror and say, "You are worth fighting for."

I was one of those kids who never had anyone cheering for me from the stands. Whether it was cheerleading competitions, basketball games, swim meets, or fashion shows, I always showed up for others, but there was no one there for me. I didn't let anyone see how much it hurt; how lonely I felt when no one was there to cheer me on. I made it through those moments, but deep down I longed for someone to just show up for me the way I always showed up for others.

When I became a mother, I promised myself that my children would never feel the way I did. Despite the exhaustion, despite my own struggles, I showed up for them every single time. My daughter, who was a cheerleader and volleyball player, always had me in the stands, cheering louder than anyone else. My oldest son, who struggled with both football and basketball, could always count on me to be there, applauding him like he was the MVP. Even when both of my sons had games at the same time, I made it work. I was there for every practice, every game, every moment that mattered. I did it all, even when I was tired, because I knew how much it would mean to them.

I know I'm not perfect. I've made plenty of mistakes. I've messed up, made decisions I regret, hurt people I loved, and let them down. But that doesn't define me. It doesn't make me a bad person. It simply makes me human. We all make mistakes. We all fall short sometimes. But that doesn't change who we are at the core.

One of the hardest lessons I learned was how to separate myself from the drama of others. Growing up in a dysfunctional family, I was often caught in the middle. If my sister had an issue with someone, I was expected to pick a side. If there was conflict, I felt like I had to be involved. But I learned I don't have to get involved in every issue, especially when it doesn't directly involve me. I learned the importance of being neutral, of protecting my own peace.

This wasn't easy. People who've known me my whole life still don't fully understand me. They don't get how I can stay out of the mess, how I can keep my distance. But I've realized that my peace is more important than being dragged into someone else's chaos. My family's struggles, their unresolved issues—they aren't mine to carry. I've spent too much of my life carrying other people's burdens, trying to fix things that weren't mine to fix. It's taken me a long time to understand I can still love my family without absorbing their problems.

As time went on, I realized no matter how hard I worked or how much money I made, my financial situation would never improve until I took control of it. But it wasn't just about the money; it was about the mindset. I had to reframe how I viewed finances, how I viewed success, and how I viewed myself in the process. I had to learn that wealth isn't just about earning money; it's about managing it wisely, making thoughtful decisions, and knowing the value of delayed gratification.

I took the lessons I learned during my first experience buying a car and applied them to my life in the years that followed. Slowly but surely, I began to rebuild my credit, live within my means, and make better financial choices. It wasn't easy, and there were setbacks along the way, but I realized each step forward was a victory. I was learning, growing, and finally taking responsibility for my financial future.

There were still times when I struggled, when it felt like things were never going to change, but I kept reminding myself that I had a choice. I could continue to repeat the same cycle, or I could change the narrative and set myself up for a future where I wasn't drowning in debt—where I could build something better for myself and my family.

It was only in my later years I understood the true importance of financial literacy. No one ever really taught me how to manage money properly. I had to learn it on my own, through trial and error, and with the help of a few people who genuinely wanted to see me succeed. But I'm grateful for those lessons, painful as they were. They forced me to grow, to think more carefully about my choices, and to prioritize my financial well-being.

I still have work to do. Financial freedom is a long-term goal, one that requires consistent effort and discipline. But I'm no longer overwhelmed by the weight of past mistakes. I now know financial hardship doesn't define me; it's how I handle it, how I rise above it, and how I make better decisions moving forward that will truly shape my future.

As I reflect on the journey that's brought me to this point, I realize that it's not about perfection—it's about progress. Every lesson learned, every mistake made, every step forward is a part of the person I am becoming. The road ahead may still have its bumps, but I now walk with a sense of purpose, ready to face whatever comes next. I've learned true growth comes when we embrace who we are, face our past, and make deliberate choices for a better future.

CLOSING PRAYER

God,

Teach me how to love from a place of healing, not hurt. Break every pattern that doesn't reflect Your design for my life. Restore what was damaged, renew what was lost, and let love in my life be led by Your wisdom.

In Jesus' name,
Amen

THE WEIGHT I CARRIED

A Living Reflection of My Grandmother— and the Parts of Her That Live in Me

She's still carrying it. And now I see that I am, too.

We don't always talk about it, but it's there. In her walk. In her prayers. In the way she still tries to protect and provide, even at her age.

She is the one everyone calls. The one who always finds a way. The one who never complains—even when it's too much.

And somehow, I became her.

For years, I thought I was just strong because life forced me to be. I thought I was holding my family together because someone had to. I thought it was just survival.

But now, I know: it's her spirit in me.

She has always been the backbone of our family. And now, I find myself becoming the same for mine.

We are two generations of women carrying weight we didn't always choose—but carrying it with grace. She taught me, without saying much, what it means to keep going when others stop. To love when it hurts. To give when you feel empty.

I see her weariness sometimes, even when she hides it behind a smile. And I feel my own, too. But I wear it like armor—because that's what she showed me.

The truth is, I've been walking in her footsteps for years without even realizing it. I'm only now recognizing the fullness of who she is—and who I've become because of her.

She's still carrying the weight.

And so am I.

But now, I carry it with more understanding.

With more intention.

With more love.

Because the weight we carry isn't just struggle—it's legacy.

And I will honor it every single day.

> *"She is clothed with strength and dignity; she can laugh at the days to come."—Proverbs 31:25*

Interlude

NO MORE SHRINKING MYSELF

For a long time, I kept editing my story—softening the truth, skipping the messy parts—just to make other people comfortable.

I didn't even realize it at first. But there I was again, prioritizing other people's comfort over my own truth. Shrinking myself to make others feel better.

I've spent so much of my life doing that—making my pain easier to digest, dimming my light to avoid making anyone uncomfortable. And for what?

So they could stay comfortable while I stayed stuck?

Not anymore.

Some people won't agree with how I lived. Some won't understand the choices I made or how I chose to heal. And that's okay.

This story isn't for their comfort. It's for my freedom.

It doesn't have to make sense to anyone else. It's not supposed to.

This story is mine—unfiltered, unedited, and finally free.

And I'm telling it now, without apology.

REFLECTION

I once mistook attention for affection and vows for validation. But healing taught me love doesn't fix brokenness; it honors wholeness. I had to learn how to be a wife by first becoming a whole woman.

CLOSING PRAYER

God,

I've stood at many crossroads—torn between who I was and who I'm becoming. Sometimes I chose fear. Sometimes I chose faith. But You never left me. When I couldn't see the road ahead, You lit the next step. Help me keep choosing forward. Help me keep choosing You.

Even when the path is hard, I trust that You're leading me to wholeness.

In Jesus' name,
Amen

Chapter 6

SILENT SUFFERING

<><><><><><><><>

*"The loudest pain is often the one no one hears.
I suffered in silence because I was too afraid to
inconvenience anyone with my breaking."*

<><><><><><><><>

I've almost been raped twice—once by one of my sister's close friends, and once by a leasing consultant.

The first time, I was home alone. My sister wasn't there, and all her friends knew it. When I heard a knock on the door, I wasn't expecting company. Still, I looked through the peephole and saw someone I recognized—my sister's friend. I had no reason to feel unsafe. After all, he was someone she trusted. I opened the door.

He asked if my sister was home.

I said, "No, but I'll let her know you came by."

I began closing the door when he suddenly shoved his foot between it and the frame. I was stunned. I asked him what he was doing.

"I see the way you look at me when I'm around," he said.

Confused and frightened, I told him, "I don't know what you're talking about. Please leave."

He ignored me, forced the door open, and pushed his way inside. The couch was near the door, and he tried to bend me over it. I fought back hard, but he was strong and deliberate in his movements. He held me down like he had done it before.

I managed to bring both my knees to his chest and flipped us over the couch. I tried to get up, but he was fast—too fast. He was on me again in seconds. I screamed at him, "If you don't get off me, I'm going to tell my sister."

That's when he stopped, pulled out his gun and said go ahead she won't believe you. And then he left.

I was devastated. I wrestled with whether I should tell my sister. I knew it would crush her, and at the time, I loved her too much to hurt her that way. I chose silence. But that silence haunted me. I cried almost every day.

Decades later—thirty years to be exact—my sister and I were catching up on the phone when she casually mentioned his name. I always hated when she talked about him, like nothing had happened. But this time, I couldn't hold it in.

I interrupted and said, "I don't mean any disrespect, but please take what I'm about to say the way I intend to give it. I really wish you wouldn't mention him when we talk."

She agreed, but then something unexpected happened. We ended up having the conversation we should have had all those years ago. I told her everything. She told me what he had told her—that I had come on to him, said all kinds of things about what I liked sexually.

I was stunned. "Why would I ever say anything like that to him?" I asked her. "I didn't even like him. I never found him attractive."

She admitted that since I'd never told her my side, and since she knew the sexual details he gave were accurate—details he must've gotten from someone I once dated—she believed him.

It all made sense now. That man was friends with someone I had previously dated. I guess they talked, shared intimate details, and he thought he'd test them out on me. But he didn't expect me to fight back. And I did—fiercely.

I carried the weight of that trauma for over thirty years. But today, I can say I've healed. I forgave my sister for believing him. I forgave myself for staying silent. I no longer feel like a victim when I speak about it—I feel like a survivor.

The second time it happened; I was looking at an apartment. The leasing consultant seemed professional, polite, even charming. He gave me a tour of the amenities, then walked me through one of the available units.

At the end of the tour, just as I was about to thank him, he grabbed me by the neck and began choking me.

But what he didn't know was that I had just completed mandatory self-defense training at work. Instinct kicked in. I stomped on his foot as hard as I could, kneed him in the groin, then brought my arm down with all my strength onto both of his hands, breaking his grip. I pushed him away and kicked him again for good measure.

Then I ran.

I sprinted to the rental office, hoping to find someone—anyone—who could help. But he was the only leasing agent working that weekend.

When I reported the incident to the property manager, her response cut deep. She looked at me and said, "That's a serious allegation. Do you have any proof?"

That's exactly why I kept it all to myself. Unless it happens to them, most people don't believe you. And even if they do, they often place the blame on you. So, I did what I'd always done—I put it in a box with all the other trauma I had learned to suppress.

I changed gradually. People don't like when you change. They expect you to stay the same. But growth requires discomfort. And just because someone is related to you doesn't mean they're connected to you. DNA doesn't make someone family. We don't get to choose the family we're born into, but we do get to decide who we keep around.

Sometimes, we have to love people back to life, especially when they're broken. I know because my husband did that for me. He loved me past my pain—twice. He stood by me until I could gather the pieces of my shattered heart.

Some wounds are loud—they scream, they rage, they demand to be seen. But the worst wounds are the ones you suffer in silence. The ones you carry alone. The ones that no one sees, but that threaten to destroy you from the inside out. This is the chapter of the battles no one knew I was fighting. The pain I buried. The parts of me I almost lost forever.

On the outside, I wore a smile. I laughed when I was supposed to, showed up when needed, and carried on like everything was fine. But inside, there was a different story—one that few, if any, knew. I became a master at hiding my pain, pushing it down so deep that sometimes even I forgot it was there. Silent suffering became a way of life. I learned how to be strong for everyone else while silently breaking under the weight of my own unspoken wounds. There were nights when the loneliness was unbearable, mornings when it took everything in me just to get out of bed and face another day.

But still, I smiled. Still, I carried on.

There are pains you scream about, and then there are the ones you carry so deep that you forget how to cry. For me, it was the second kind—silent, heavy, invisible. I walked through life smiling, laughing, showing up for others, while silently bleeding inside.

My pain had layers.

Pain from broken relationships. Pain from my father being absent, building a life with other children while I stood on the outside looking in. Pain from losing my brother—not just in death, but long before that, losing him to the streets, to jail, to a life that swallowed him whole before murder took him the rest of the way. Some subjects are off limits in my life, and my baby brother is one of them.

The life he lived and the man he was to me are two very different things. I'm not blind to the choices he made, but they don't define the memories I hold close. I won't allow anyone—not even reality itself—to tarnish what he meant to me. My memories of him are what carried me through some of the darkest nights of my life. For a long time, I suffered with survivor's remorse. When my brother was murdered, the light that burned inside me went out. The one person who loved me—with his whole heart, without conditions—was gone. And with him, I lost my anchor. I was adrift, desperate, afraid.

How could I navigate this life without him? Without his laughter, his wisdom, his presence? Would I turn back into that helpless little girl I was before he became my protector? Who would shield me now?

I was vulnerable again—exposed—and I hated the fear that crept back into my spirit. I wondered if the predators could smell it on me now that he was gone. I was mad at the world, furious at the injustice, as if the earth itself owed me his life. I couldn't function under the weight of my grief. Every morning for four years, we had a ritual.

Before our days began, before the noise of the world could interrupt us, we would talk. No matter where he was headed, no matter what was waiting for him—he made time for me. Every call ended the same way, "I love you." He wasn't a man who wore his heart on his sleeve for just anyone, but for me he made an exception.

I was his safe place, just as he was mine. When my baby brother died, a piece of me died with him. I became a hollow version of myself—a zombie trapped in a nightmare I couldn't wake up from.

I barely noticed when my marriage crumbled, when my daughter moved away. I lived in a daze for five long years, drowning silently inside my own life. It wasn't until I found out I was pregnant with my son that something shifted. For the first time in years, I had a reason to choose life over death. I decided—not easily, not quickly—but I decided I wanted to get busy living, or I would continue dying.

Grief had trapped me in a vicious cycle. I didn't want it to be real. I couldn't accept it. Not my brother. Not him. Antidepressants, sleeping pills, Ativan—they numbed the pain, but they also numbed me. I spent so many days at the cemetery, sometimes sleeping there because it felt closer to him than my own home.

I wasn't in my right mind, and in some ways, maybe I never truly came back. Because losing him wasn't just losing my brother—it was losing the one person who saw me, the one person who understood the sadness I carried long before either of us had the words to name it.

He was my protector, my life coach, my personal trainer, my father when I needed one, my counselor when I was broken. He was all of that and more. The loss of my brother is something I'll never be able to describe fully. I didn't recover from it. I learned how to survive it, but I never truly healed.

And then, my godson. This loss cut deep in a way that still feels raw. He was only 19, just a baby to me. Gone far too soon. Grief doesn't look the same on everyone. Just because someone doesn't grieve the way you think they should doesn't mean they aren't hurting.

Grief has no rulebook. It has no timeline. And it certainly doesn't ask for permission to destroy you from the inside out. I am a living testament to that. I carry my scars quietly, but they run deep.

I smile, but behind the smile is a battlefield most people will never see. And every day, I choose to keep living—not because I'm unbroken, but because somewhere deep inside me, the love they gave me still fights to keep me alive.

Pain from losing my father to women and drugs, long before life ever had a chance to change him. Pain from losing my mother to men and to everything and everyone else she seemed to care about more. Pain from being the baby sister who never had a chance—trying to love my big sister, but never being chosen in return. Pain because he was right about her and she was wrong about me. Pain because she didn't believe me knowing that I would never lie.

I really looked up to my big sister. She let me down and broke my heart all at the same time. She never apologized. She just started talking to me like nothing had ever happened—like the heartbreak, the betrayal, the silent wounds didn't exist.

Pain makes people change, but I didn't change all at once. It took me 27 long, emotional years to finally be done with it. Pain because I wanted her validation so badly that I abandoned the spirituality I had known all my life, just to win her approval.

I lost my connection with God chasing a connection with her, and even that wasn't enough. I was treated in ways that made me question my worth, made me doubt the value of my soul. I sacrificed pieces of myself trying to be accepted. But in the end, all I lost was myself. And still—even in that loss—I found freedom. Sometimes, choosing yourself is the only way to survive.

Pain because my younger brother always went against the grain and could never be loyal, no matter how much I wanted to believe otherwise.

Pain from being a giver, pouring myself out for people who rarely poured back into me.

Pain from suffering a miscarriage while quietly celebrating others' blessings, hiding my own grief behind a smile.

Pain because I idolized and looked up to her and she chose him. Pain because I always thought it was my fault.

Pain because she said I had a dead womb and would never bare children.

Pain of inadequacy, the deep ache of never feeling like I was enough, no matter how hard I tried.

Pain because I kept showing up for people who didn't even notice when I was drowning.

Pain from watching my godson lose his battle, standing helplessly as life slipped away.

Pain from watching my nephew struggle with addiction, feeling powerless to save him.

Pain because I remained silent when I should have spoken up.

Pain because I knew I was wrong but didn't make it right.

Pain because I self-sabotage and didn't know how to move out my own way.

Pain from passing my own dysfunction down to my children, even though all I wanted was to shelter them from it. And then there was the pain that came from a different kind of loss. The kind where you lose someone long before they ever die.

My sister and I hadn't spoken in eleven years before she passed away. I buried my feelings for her so deep that when the time came, I didn't shed a single tear—not until they started to close the casket. It was in that moment, watching them lower her away from this world, that I realized I had lost a sibling, not a sister.

I shed some tears that day but that was it. Whatever feelings I had left were buried with her. I had released her the day I mailed her that final letter; she released me the day she was buried. There's no regret in my heart.

I made the decision to close that door for my own peace, and I stand by it. Unapologetically. Grief comes in many forms. Sometimes it's the crushing, suffocating kind that leaves you gasping for air. And sometimes, it's the quiet acceptance that certain relationships had already died long before the body did.

In the end, it wasn't about anger. It wasn't about revenge. It was about survival. And survival demanded that I choose myself—even when it hurt. Losing her was a different kind of death—the death of expectation, of hope, of all the silent prayers I once whispered for our relationship. But it wasn't the only loss I carried.

There were other wounds, deeper scars, heavier griefs that shaped me just as much—if not more. And some of that pain, I would carry for the rest of my life. Don't get me wrong, I still love and care for my family. I always will. But now, I love and care for myself more. I carried it all in silence, believing if I could just hold on a little longer, maybe things would change. Maybe love would finally find me in the way I had always craved. But what I didn't understand back then was that true healing doesn't come from waiting for others to change.

It comes from facing the pain, owning it, feeling it, and deciding that it will no longer define you. God had to allow me to be broken so that I could walk in my purpose. It wasn't punishment—it was preparation.

Back Down Memory Lane

Come take a walk with me down memory lane—back to a time when being a kid was our only job. No cell phones, no iPads, no smart-watches, no Xbox, no PlayStation, or Nintendo Switch. We didn't even have color TVs. Just those old-model black-and-white sets with a wire hanger twisted into place for the antenna and a pair of pliers sitting nearby to change the channel because the knob was long gone.

But let me tell you, Saturday morning cartoons on that TV were everything. We'd wake up early, still in our pajamas, with a bowl of cereal in hand—Froot Loops, Cookie Crisp, Apple Jacks, Honey Combs or Cornflakes, depending on what Mama could get on sale—and plop down on the carpet like it was front-row seating at the movies. There was no pause button, no rewind, no streaming—if you missed it, you missed it. So, we watched every second with wide eyes and open hearts.

Outside, we created our own kind of magic. Dirt became race-tracks for our wildest races, sticks turned into mighty swords in back-yard battles, and a jump rope was all we needed for hours of laughter, rhythm, and double dutch showdowns. We didn't need toys that lit up or talked back—just each other, a bit of imagination, and the freedom to run wild until the streetlights blinked on, signaling it was time to head home.

It was a simpler time, but somehow it felt richer—richer in joy, louder with belly laughs, and fuller with the kind of love that came without conditions. Life moved slower back then, and maybe that's why those moments etched themselves so deeply into my heart.

After school didn't mean homework and stress—it meant playtime. No thoughts of bills, burdens, or grown-up worries. We were just kids, free to live in the moment. The whole neighborhood would come alive as we gathered on the sidewalks and front yards, playing games like hopscotch, red light green light, hide and seek, 7-Eleven, Jacks, freeze tag, and of course Simon Says. But my all-time favorite? Rockin' Robin. The beat, the clapping, the joy—it was more than a game. It was our anthem, our rhythm, our shared heartbeat during the golden hours of childhood.

We grew up on mayonnaise, syrup, and sugar sandwiches, hot dogs straight out the pack, bologna with the red string, and plain Corn Flakes with no sugar. We drank Kool-Aid and Tang like it was fine wine. If one kid had a bike, we all took turns riding it. Same for skates—those heavy metal ones that sparked up the sidewalk. We had Huffy bikes, pogo sticks, Sit & Spins, and Green Machines. And when the fire hydrant opened up on hot summer days? That was our water park.

The ice cream truck always pulled up at the right time, like it knew when joy was peaking. We'd hear the music blocks away, run in to ask Grandma for change, then bolt back outside for swirl cones, Lemonheads, Alexander grapes, Chico Sticks, Pop Rocks, Sugar Babies, and those ten-pack gumballs.

Those were the good old days—before life got complicated. Back then, joy was simple, shared, and pure.

REFLECTION

The silent suffering almost broke me. It clawed at my spirit and shattered pieces of who I once was. It buried parts of me alive, one by one, until there were days I couldn't even recognize myself. Carrying that pain nearly destroyed me beyond repair, and remembering it felt like dying all over again.

But even in the silence, a warrior was being born. Bloodied, bruised, and battle-worn, I rose from the ashes—still breathing, still fighting, determined to set myself free. The suffering shaped me, but it would not define me. I wasn't created just to endure—I was created to overcome.

Survival wasn't enough anymore. I came for my freedom. What tried to destroy me only taught me how to survive with fire in my veins. The girl who suffered is gone, and what remains is a woman who survived herself. I wasn't built to break—I was built to burn down everything that tried to bury me. From shattered pieces, I built the strongest version of me.

I am no longer my pain. I am my own victory. I am no longer who the world tried to make me. I am who I decided to become.

And yet, even in my strength, I was surrounded but felt alone—loud rooms, quiet soul. Deep down, I knew I couldn't keep carrying this silently forever.

CLOSING PRAYER

God,

I've mastered the art of looking fine while falling apart. I've smiled through pain, stayed strong in silence, and hid what hurt the most. But You saw every tear I cried behind closed doors. I'm tired of carrying it alone. Teach me to find healing in honesty and strength in surrender. Let my silence turn into testimony.

Amen

Chapter 7

BREAKING THE CHAINS

◇◇◇◇◇◇◇◇◇◇

*"The chains didn't fall all at once. But the moment
I chose myself, the lock began to loosen."*

◇◇◇◇◇◇◇◇◇◇

After going through therapy, I came face to face with something I had buried deep for years—I was just as angry at my mother as I was at my father. The difference? She stayed. She was present. She watched it all go down. And in some ways, that made it worse.

My mother never pretended to be someone she wasn't. She didn't sugarcoat her failures. Truthfully, I don't think she even cared at the time. I'll never forget the day she finally said the words out loud, "I wasn't a good mother." I didn't have children yet, but my sister did. And my mother turned to her and said, "You're already a better mother than I ever was." That moment cut through me. The weight in her voice. The regret in her tone. The sorrow in her eyes. It was one of the rare times I saw the little girl inside her beaten down by her own guilt and mistakes.

Therapy forced me to look inward before reaching outward. My therapist told me healing had to start with me. I had to forgive myself first—for the ways I showed up broken, for the times I let pain speak louder than love, for the chaos I kept calling normal. Only then could I begin to sort through the ruins of my relationships.

But here's the truth: not everything broken is meant to be fixed.

Some relationships are too toxic to touch again. Some are frozen in time—no matter how much you want to thaw them. Some remain strained, tugging at the soul with silent tension. And some... they simply are what they are. Whatever that means for your peace.

I've reached a place where I can love you from a distance or not at all. I've made peace with the possibility of healing without reconciliation. I've cleared my circle of the dead weight: the negative, the judgmental, the manipulative, the ones who smile with their mouths but curse you in their hearts.

Letting go didn't just free me—it saved me. And my life? It's quieter now. But it's also fuller. Healthier. Realer. I finally understand: peace isn't the absence of people. It's the presence of self.

Breaking the chains wasn't a single moment of victory—it was a thousand small rebellions against everything that once tried to keep me bound.

I had to unlearn survival tactics that had kept me trapped. I had to confront the parts of myself shaped by pain, fear, and betrayal—the parts that believed I wasn't worthy of real love, real peace, or real happiness.

For a long time, I thought loyalty meant staying, even when staying was killing me. I thought love meant enduring, even when enduring was breaking my spirit.

But I finally understood real love—whether from family, friends, or even myself—doesn't demand my silence, my suffering, or my self-betrayal.

Breaking the chains meant choosing myself, unapologetically.

It meant setting boundaries that people didn't understand. It meant grieving the version of me who tolerated less because she didn't know she deserved more. It meant walking away from patterns, relationships, and environments that no longer aligned with the future I was fighting for.

Every chain I broke brought me closer to the woman I was born to be: Not a prisoner of her past, but the architect of her future.

I didn't just survive what was meant to destroy me—I rose and reclaimed my life, piece by piece, breath by breath.

This time, I wasn't asking for permission. This time, I wasn't shrinking to make others comfortable. This time, I was stepping fully into my freedom—unbound, unbroken, and unstoppable

Breaking The Cycle

I used to talk about breaking generational curses long before I even understood the weight of those words. Back then, it just sounded powerful, something bold to say out loud. But I didn't realize how deep that statement ran until I caught myself living out the same patterns I swore I'd escape.

That's when the truth hit me: I wasn't just talking about change, I was desperate for it.

I started trying to be different, to do better. But every time I made a move in the right direction, an obstacle seemed to appear. My family is known for having vicious attitudes—and that's not a rumor, it's reality. I won't pretend otherwise. I've had to wrestle with my own attitude, and while I manage it most days, some days people really do push you past your breaking point.

I've walked away from more jobs than I care to count because of my temper. Disrespect is something I simply don't tolerate. I don't care what position you hold—title, rank, or power. I'll give you respect, but not at the expense of my own. I refuse to be talked down to or made to feel small. There's no need to lead with fear or arrogance when you can lead with love and respect—and still get results. The truth is, not everyone is fit to lead, not everyone can manage, and not every teacher was born to teach.

Let me be real with you: If I feel like you'll lead me into battle just to watch me fall, I won't follow. If you're my manager and don't know how to manage, I won't fall in line.

And if you're my teacher and you can't teach, I will drop your class.

I've learned to trust myself. "Going along to get along" got me into more trouble than I can explain—like being promoted just so I could be the one to fire people others were too afraid to confront. Or watching someone let their new title change who they were when just last week we were on the same level.

I'm all for growth—but not at the cost of my character. I won't stab anyone in the back to get ahead. My integrity is intact. I am a woman of my word. And I don't make promises I can't keep.

Interlude

---◇◈◇◈◇---

FIRE AND GRACE

I didn't ask for it, but it came anyway—passed down like a family heirloom no one wanted but everyone carried. My mother's attitude was fierce, sharp like a knife, and just as quick to cut. She had a tongue that could light a room on fire and a stare that made grown folks shrink back. And somewhere along the way, without even realizing it, I became her echo.

My attitude was so vicious that people thought I was unapproachable. They'd whisper about me before ever speaking to me. I'd walk into a room, and the air would shift—not because of confidence, but because of caution. People didn't greet me; they braced for me. And honestly, that used to make me feel powerful. I thought if people feared me, they couldn't hurt me. I thought being intimidating meant I had control. But deep down, I was just scared of being vulnerable.

I remember one job where my name was known before my face. The manager pulled me aside during my first week and said, "I heard you don't take no mess." She meant it as a warning, not a compliment. I laughed it off, but I knew what she was really saying: We're watching you. I didn't even get the chance to be known for my work—just for my attitude. I wore that label like armor. Cold. Short. Dismissive.

But being unapproachable doesn't protect you—it isolates you. When you act like you don't need anyone, eventually no one shows up. And when life got hard, when I was spiraling, when I needed help—all that toughness didn't keep me warm. It just kept me alone.

Then came my husband—and let me be clear, he wasn't gentle at first. He was an alpha male through and through—bold, proud, and unshaken. And me? I was an alpha female, raised to defend myself before I was ever taught how to receive love. We were fire meeting fire. Passionate, intense, and stubborn to the core.

There were nights we slept in separate rooms—not because we needed space, but because we were both too stubborn to surrender. It wasn't silence that filled the air, it was war. A quiet kind of war—one where no one raised their voice, but everything screamed. Unspoken words stacked up like bricks until we built a wall we couldn't see over.

We separated at least three times. I had a toxic pattern I didn't recognize back then. "Get out!" I'd shout whenever I was angry, overwhelmed, or hurting. That was my go-to weapon. Those words came out like bullets. And his pride? His ego? They never let him stay. So, he left over and over again. And every time, I told myself I was done. I acted like I didn't care. I wore my pain like armor.

But the truth? Each time he walked out that door, a piece of me shattered. I cried in rooms no one saw. I begged God to fix what I was too broken to hold together. I never really wanted him to leave—I just didn't know how to ask him to stay. That was how I handled conflict back then: push away what I was afraid to lose. Destroy what I didn't know how to heal.

Still... somehow, he always came back. And deep down, I think I was always waiting at the door, hoping he would. Not because we didn't have other options, but because, despite it all, we were drawn to each other in a way we couldn't explain. Something deeper than the arguments, louder than the silence, stronger than our egos pulled us back together every time.

It wasn't just love—it was a bond. A knowing. Like God kept stitching us back together, thread by thread until we finally started to understand the assignment: we weren't here to break each other. We were here to build something new.

He didn't change me overnight. And I didn't make him soft. We evolved—painfully, slowly, and sometimes stubbornly into something stronger. But I didn't truly soften, not all the way, until I got pregnant with my youngest son.

That baby shifted the atmosphere. Carrying him made me crave peace more than pride. I didn't want to yell anymore. I didn't want my child to feel the tension in the air or hear love spoken in tones that sounded like war. I wanted softness. I wanted stability. And I wanted to become a woman who could give both.

Today, my husband is an amazing father to our three children—present, loving, and intentional. He's the kind of father I prayed for before I even knew how to pray properly. He's patient where I'm fiery, calm where I'm emotional, steady where I've wavered. And he loves our children in a way that heals the parts of me that still remember what it felt like to grow up without that kind of steady presence.

He is also an amazing partner. Not perfect—but present. And in a world full of people who run at the first sign of difficulty, that kind of presence is everything. He has walked with me through nearly every storm I've faced—not just as a bystander, but as a true covering. For almost 21 years, he's stayed. Through my healing, my breaking, my re-building. Through my sharp words and silent treatments, through tears I didn't know how to explain, and battles I didn't know how to fight.

He's seen the worst parts of me and never used them as a reason to leave.

We didn't get here by chance. We got here by grace. By God's grace, we are both healed. Not the same people we once were but better. Softer. Stronger. Wiser. We've learned how to love without losing ourselves, how to fight for each other instead of with each other, and how to build a home where peace is louder than pain.

And now, when I look at my children, I see the beauty of what we've survived. I see the legacy we're shaping—not of perfection, but of perseverance. Of choosing love over and over again. Even when it's hard. Especially when it's hard.

Because this love? It was earned. It was battled for. And most of all… it was redeemed.

CLOSING PRAYER

God,

I've been bound by things I never chose—fear, shame, patterns passed down like inheritance. But I know now: what begins with You can end with me. I don't want to survive in chains—I want to live in freedom. Give me the strength to keep breaking what once held me captive.

Break every cycle that does not honor who You've called me to be. I declare: it ends with me.

In Jesus' name,
Amen

Chapter 8

SHOWING UP & SPEAKING TRUTH

◇◇◇◇◇◇◇◇◇◇

"Breaking the cycle means making daily choices that honor the future you want, not the past you survived."

◇◇◇◇◇◇◇◇◇◇

Growing up in the kind of environment—where love came with conditions, where words cut deeper than silence, and where loyalty sometimes looked like sacrifice—I learned early how to survive. But survival isn't the same as living.

Being the youngest girl meant I often played the background. I watched. I listened. I absorbed everything—how people treated each other, how anger showed up in different forms, and how some wounds weren't always visible. I thought if I could be good enough, helpful enough, quiet enough, maybe I'd earn a love that didn't feel so conditional.

It shaped how I moved in the world. I became the fixer. The peace-keeper. The one who apologized just to smooth things over, even if I wasn't wrong. I let people cross boundaries because I didn't even know I was supposed to have any. And in relationships—especially romantic ones—I confused attention with affection and chaos with passion. If someone didn't treat me right, I'd try harder. Give more. Love deeper. Until there was nothing left to give.

But over time, I realized I had spent so much of my life trying to be seen by people who only looked when they needed something. I kept showing up for folks who couldn't do the same for me. And the sad part? I thought that was normal.

I started to believe that my worth was tied to what I could offer. That if I wasn't fixing something or holding someone down, I wasn't valuable. But the truth is, I was valuable the whole time. I just didn't know it.

Breaking that cycle wasn't easy. It meant letting go of some relationships I never thought I would. It meant saying no without guilt. It meant speaking up, even if my voice shook. It meant standing alone sometimes, but choosing me every time.

And now? I walk differently. I love differently. I understand that healthy love doesn't tear you down—it builds you up. It doesn't keep score or punish you for growing. I've learned that not everyone who claims to love you knows how to love you well. And that's okay.

Because I do.

There are moments in life that shape who we are—not the big, glamorous moments, but the quiet, painful ones: the times when no one showed up, when mistakes were made, and when choices had lasting consequences. These experiences taught me lessons I carry with me to this day—lessons about showing up, speaking truthfully, and taking control of my own life, one decision at a time.

Support That Changes Everything

To every parent with a child in extracurriculars—whether it's sports, music, dance, debate, or anything in between—hear me when I say this: **show up.** Be there. Even if they're not the star player. Even if they miss every note. Even if they stumble or freeze on stage.

Be there anyway.

Your presence is louder than your praise. Your support is stronger than your silence.

Thirty years later, I'm still writing about it. Because it mattered. Because the absence of it left an ache that never quite went away. Nothing cuts deeper than looking into the crowd and not seeing your parents. Nothing stings more than wondering if they're proud of you— or worse, assuming they're not.

You may think they're too young to notice, too distracted to care, but let me tell you—they feel it all. They notice every time you don't show up. They remember every time you do.

You don't know the courage it takes for a child to try something new, to stand in front of people, to risk failing with the world watching. But when they see you—when they lock eyes with the person who's supposed to believe in them more than anyone—something shifts. Their hands stop shaking. Their heart beats steadier. They feel seen. And in that moment, they believe in themselves just a little bit more.

So please, show up. Cheer loud. Clap hard. Let them know, "I'm proud of you—not because you're perfect, but because you're trying." Your support could be the difference between them giving up… or growing wings.

Showing up doesn't require perfection—just presence. Support doesn't have to be loud or flashy; sometimes just being there says everything.

The Power And Responsibility Of My Words

I'm aware of my sharp tongue. I know it can cut deeper than intended sometimes. But here's the truth—I wasn't always like this. I used to be afraid to speak up, afraid that my words would be dismissed, twisted, or used against me. So, I stayed quiet. I swallowed my truth. I let people walk over me, talk down to me, and decide who I was. But silence has a way of building pressure. And eventually, I erupted.

Now, I speak up even when it's messy. Even when it costs me. I say what I mean and I mean what I say. It's not about being disrespectful—it's about finally refusing to be disrespected. I've spent too many years with my voice buried under fear and guilt. Now that I've found it, I'm not letting it go.

So yes, my tongue is sharp, but it's sharpened from years of being silenced. And I'd rather be loud and misunderstood than quiet and broken. But growth taught me something else too: just because I can say it doesn't mean I should. These days, I pause. I think before I speak. I've learned to be mindful of other people's feelings because healing isn't just about finding your voice, it's about learning how to use it with grace.

Choosing To Break The Cycle

Through it all, I've learned the importance of showing up—whether for my kids, my family, or myself. I learned that it's okay to be imperfect. It's okay to make mistakes. What matters most is showing up every day, learning from the past, and choosing to do better tomorrow. It's not about being perfect; it's about being present, being real, and being willing to grow.

In this chapter of my life, I finally began to stand firmly in my own identity. I said no to the patterns that kept repeating themselves. I stopped living for everyone else's expectations. I chose to be different.

I chose to break the cycle. I chose to make my own way. And while it wasn't easy, it was absolutely worth it.

Choosing A Different Future

There were times when I struggled, when it felt like nothing was ever going to change. But I kept reminding myself: I had a choice. I could continue to repeat the same cycle or I could change the narrative. I could build something better for myself and for my family.

It wasn't until later in life that I truly understood the importance of financial literacy. No one had ever taught me these things. I learned the hard way through trial and error and with the support of a few people who genuinely wanted to see me succeed. And for those hard, painful lessons, I am grateful.

My past mistakes may have shaped me, but they do not define me. I still have work to do. Financial freedom isn't something you achieve overnight; it's a long journey requiring consistent effort and discipline. But I'm no longer overwhelmed by the weight of my past mistakes.

Now, I know that financial hardship doesn't define me. How I rise above it, how I choose differently, and how I move forward—that's what defines me.

REFLECTION

1. When was a time in your life that someone simply "showing up" made all the difference for you?
2. What areas of your life are still affected by the financial lessons or the lack of them from your early years?
3. Are there patterns or cycles you're currently working to break in your own life? What motivates you to keep pushing through?
4. How do you use your voice? Are there areas where you need to be more mindful, or maybe more courageous, when you speak?
5. If you could tell your younger self one lesson about responsibility, money, or self-worth, what would it be?

Every time I showed up for myself, I rewrote a piece of my story. This was no longer about proving anything to anyone. It was about living in alignment with the woman I was always meant to be.

CLOSING PRAYER

God,

For too long I shrank myself to keep others comfortable. I silenced my truth, second-guessed my worth, and stayed hidden when You called me to rise. But no more. I'm ready to show up—as I am, healed and healing, bold and becoming. Give me the courage to speak what's true, even when my voice shakes. Help me shape a future that reflects Your glory, not my fear. Let my truth set others free, too.

In Jesus' name,
Amen

Chapter 9

FAMILY

◇◇◇◇◇◇◇◇◇◇

"I stopped needing my family to change in order for me to heal. I chose freedom—and that changed everything."

◇◇◇◇◇◇◇◇◇◇

It's a word that used to carry weight and confusion all at once. I used to think family was just blood—the people you were born to, the ones tied to you by name or obligation. But over time, through pain, growth, and healing, I've learned that family isn't always who shares your DNA—it's who shows up with love, respect, and truth.

In this chapter, I begin to peel back the layers of what "family" meant to me then and what it means to me now. I reflect on parents who were physically present, yet emotionally distant. I revisit the pain of carrying a devastating secret I kept from my sister for decades. And I honor the man who stood beside me as I gathered the shattered pieces of my heart and slowly began to heal. This is the chapter where I speak the unfiltered truth about the people who shaped me, wounded me, walked with me, and ultimately taught me the difference between being related by blood... and being held by love.

My grandmother is the matriarch of our family—a phenomenal woman, the epitome of grace, strength, and unconditional love. She is the Queen of all Queens, my Golden Girl, and truly in a class of her own. She never smoked, drank, or partied and even if she ever did, she carried herself with such poise and dignity; we never saw anything less than the example she wanted to set. I grew up watching her care for our family with unwavering devotion and quiet strength. There was nothing she wouldn't do for us. She raised her children, her grandchildren, and even her great-grandchildren—her work, her love, her presence, have always been constant.

Even as a child, I knew I wanted to grow up to be like her. Everyone adores her—my mother, my aunts and uncles, cousins, neighbors, and anyone blessed enough to cross her path.

One of the greatest feelings in the world is to be loved by my grandmother and that hasn't changed now that I'm an adult. She carries the weight of the world on her shoulders, yet still walks with her head held high. She holds our family's secrets, heals our wounds, and keeps us stitched together with her strength. She is the glue—the heart—of our family.

She didn't just raise a family—she built a legacy of love, one heart at a time.

I was terrified of my mother. She ruled with an iron fist—her way or the highway, no exceptions. She protected us the best way she knew how. We always had a roof over our heads, clothes on our backs, and food on the table. But anything beyond that feels like a blur.

My mother was the type to "whoop first, ask questions later." If you did something you had no business doing, you better believe there were going to be consequences—and fast. She didn't wait around for explanations or lies. Looking back, I now understand that when a parent asks if you did something, it's usually because they already know the answer. They just want to see if you'll tell the truth.

I used to think my mother was crazy. She cursed like a sailor and had no filter—none. It seemed like she was always caught up in a dispute, an argument, or some kind of fight. As a child, I didn't understand it. I just knew it didn't feel normal.

But now, as a mother myself, I see things differently. I realize that she carried wounds of her own—pain she never had the tools or space to heal from. Her love was tough because life had been tough on her. And while I didn't always feel emotionally safe growing up, I've made it my mission to break that cycle. I want my children to know that love isn't just about survival—it's also about softness, patience, and being seen. That's how healing begins.

My friends feared my mother, too. They were scared to call our house, let alone come over. When I wanted to hang out, I met them at the playground instead. My mother had a reputation. She was the kind of woman who showed up when you called her. You know those moments when a kid gets bold, and you say, "Go get your mama?" Well, my mama showed up ready for anything. Most of the time, the other parent wasn't ready for her.

The apple definitely fell far from the tree. My mother was nothing like my grandmother. I guess she inherited her behavior from her father instead. Looking back, I'm almost certain I had childhood PTSD. My anxiety was sky-high because I was constantly afraid of doing anything outside the lines. I lived in fear of punishment, never really feeling safe enough to express myself.

That's not to say I didn't have good moments growing up—I did. But I was broken long before I even understood what that meant. I suffered in silence. I didn't know how to express my feelings, and I definitely didn't know how to communicate with my mother. Fear kept me quiet, and confusion kept me stuck. She was who she was, and I was afraid of the unknown.

There are no perfect parents, just like there are no perfect children. I often wish life came with a manual—maybe then things would have been easier. But it doesn't, so we learn as we go.

Oh, and when it comes to cooking? That gene skipped my mama. Sorry, Ma, but cooking just wasn't your thing! Don't get me wrong, she had a few signature dishes: goulash, neck bones and rice, fried fish, and her seafood salad. But that was about it. Love you anyway... just not for the food! LOL.

There was this one time I wanted to skip school to go to Dunbar High School's homecoming. All my friends were going, and I didn't want to be left out. I asked my mother if I could go, and she hit me with a flat-out, "No, take your ass to school." I said, "Okay," but I already had a plan. I waited for her to leave for work, then I doubled back into the house, got dressed, and headed to homecoming like nothing happened. I had a great time, too—laughing, dancing, living it up like a normal teenager.

What I didn't know was that my mother was playing chess while I was playing checkers. She let me think I'd gotten away with it. I came home later that day with my "I've-been-at-school" face on, and there she was—waiting at the door. Arms crossed. Calm, but deadly.

"So, you went to the homecoming anyway?" she asked.

I knew better than to lie. When your mama asks you something like that, she already knows the answer. I said, "Yes."

She nodded. "So, you going to do what you want to do, huh?"

I said, "No, ma'am."

She said, "Well, since you're going to do what you want to do, I'm going to do what I want to do too. You're punished. For a year."

I looked at her like she had lost her mind. "Did you say a year?" I asked, hoping I'd misheard.

She looked me dead in the eye and said, "You heard me right. One year."

Now, I was a teenager. I figured after a couple of weeks she'd cool off and let it go. Nope. She stood ten toes down. I was punished for a whole year. The only place I was allowed to go was school and straight back home. No phone, no friends, no fun.

After a while, I think even she got tired of me sitting in the house looking pitiful. She eventually told me, "Get out of my face and go outside."

When my mother said something, she meant it. I thought she was crazy. She told me I was being punished for a year because I had the nerve to ask her for permission and then disobey her. She said if I had just skipped school without asking, I still would've been punished, but not for a whole year. I understood her logic... kind of. But a full year? That felt extreme, at least to me.

The first time I ever truly rebelled against my mother was Ie of one of my cousins. For some reason, this girl could do no wrong in my mother's eyes. I swear she came out the womb with a mission to start drama. I never cared too much for her, even when we were little. One day, completely unprovoked, she spit in my face, just because she felt like it. I smacked her so hard she screamed.

My mother came running. She didn't ask any questions, didn't care about what led up to the moment. She just saw my cousin crying and holding her face... and she slapped me so hard I spun in a full circle.

That was the day I told my mother I hated her... and packed my things to move in with my grandmother along with everybody else who took refuge there. Of course, I didn't really mean it. I was just hurt. I couldn't believe she hit me like that without even asking what happened, especially knowing how messy that little girl could be.

Back then, my mom used to send me to the store with a handwritten list and a booklet of food stamps. There were no EBT cards—just the colorful stamps, torn from a little paper book. She never let us get anything extra. But if my sister came with me, she would always spend the change. She'd say, "If Ma asks, just tell her I spent it." But she'd never walk back home with me. Her excuse? "I'm the one who got the stamps for us anyway."

I was terrified to go home without that change. I just knew my mother was going to kill me. But I did as my sister told me and threw her under the bus. When my mom asked where the change was, I said your daughter spent it. She'd just glare at me and say, "But I gave the stamps to you." I'd stand there like a deer in headlights. Somehow, she always let me off the hook. But I never knew what kind of day she was having and when she might finally snap. So, I stayed out of her way.

My mama definitely had a loose screw. I don't even remember us having showers back then. One day, my boyfriend came by to visit. I let him in and told him to wait while I went upstairs for a quick bath. I couldn't have been gone long, but by the time I came back down, all hell had broken loose.

My boyfriend was outside tied to the lamp post in front of our house... wearing my mother's bathrobe.

To this day, I have no idea what he did or said in those few minutes while I was upstairs. All I know is, she took his clothes and tied him to that pole. Who even does that?

REFLECTION

Looking back, I realize my childhood was a mixture of chaos and survival. I grew up learning how to tiptoe around triggers, how to lie to protect myself, and how to bury emotions that had no place in a house where fear ruled more than love. My mother did what she knew. She parented from her own pain, passed down like an heirloom. But even in the confusion and dysfunction, I see now that she was doing the best she could with what life handed her.

I didn't always feel safe, but I did feel shaped. Not in all the ways I wanted, but in ways that taught me strength, discernment, and resilience. And somehow, even in the trauma, I still searched for connection. I still wanted to be seen. I still hoped for peace.

As I got older, I realized that survival wasn't enough. I wanted healing. And healing starts with honesty. So, this is me telling the truth... not to blame, but to break the cycle.

I wasn't physically abused as a child, but I lived it. I witnessed it. And sometimes, I was pulled into it. There were times when, while one of my siblings was getting a whooping, I was enlisted to help hold them down so they wouldn't escape in the process. It traumatized me because if I refused or let go too soon, I knew I would be next.

What hurt even more was that my siblings didn't always seem to care or at least they pretended not to. I cried many nights for them, especially my baby brother. He was the most innocent of us all, the true baby of the family. People often assume the youngest child is the most spoiled, but in our house, that wasn't the case.

When you know better, you do better. My mother may not have been Mother Teresa, but she's a wonderful grandmother. She doesn't hold back her love and affection when it comes to her grandchildren—though she'll still whoop your ass, now she does it with love. Healing doesn't mean the damage never existed. It means the damage no longer controls our lives. My mother and I have been through a lot, but today I'm honored to say she is the wind beneath my wings.

My father abused drugs for most of my life. He was, for the most part, nonexistent. His absence left a void I didn't know how to fill. He was the reason I went searching for love in every man I met. Without his guidance, I had no example of what to look for in a man—no blueprint, no protection, no fatherly wisdom to help me avoid the knuckleheads.

When I met my first boyfriend, I was clueless. I didn't know what love was supposed to look like. I needed my father. I was a little girl with a heart full of questions and no one to answer them. As the years passed, the unanswered questions turned into bitterness. The older I got, the more that bitterness took root.

I didn't grow up watching healthy relationships. What I saw was dysfunction, and that's exactly how my relationships began. I didn't know there was another way because I had nothing else to compare it to.

My father would show up from time to time, but those moments were few and far between. When he did come around, he was usually full of excuses and empty promises—words that felt broken before they even left his mouth. Still, I held onto every one of them... until the day I didn't.

By then, I had built up a wall of anger. I was mean to him when he came around. I couldn't help it—I was angry. Some moments between us were okay, even tender. But when he would ask me what my problem was, I would say, "Does it matter? Are you going to fix it?" He'd just look at me with sad eyes, as if he knew I was right.

I remember one moment clearly. I was around 23, and my sister was having an event at her place. My father was there. I can't recall what the topic of conversation was, but at one point he jumped in and said, "Daughter, you shouldn't do that, you should do this..." trying to offer advice. I completely spazzed out. I looked at him and said, "You don't get to have a say in my life. Honestly, you should've pulled out and let the sperm hit the sheets if you were going to be a deadbeat."

At the time, I didn't see it as disrespectful. I saw it as truth. But now, with maturity and hindsight, I know how hurtful those words were. I saw the pain in his eyes, but I didn't care. Not then. He had hurt me my entire life, and I didn't think he deserved my grace. The saddest part is, he had no idea how deep my hurt ran because he hadn't been there to see it.

Yes, he showed up sometimes—if I chased him down, popped up at his job, or found him at home. If I asked him to do something, he would usually come through. But he was never present in the way I needed. I was so angry that I didn't even call him "Dad." I called him by his first name. And honestly, I can't remember a time when I called him anything else.

Still, despite all that pain and all those broken pieces, there were three significant moments when he did show up for me. He was there for my high school graduation. He was there for my wedding reception—and not just as a guest, he catered it. And he was there when I was seriously ill and hospitalized for a month. He visited me at least three times a week, not because I asked, but because he wanted to. That mattered more than he knew.

I was surprised the first time my father visited me in the hospital, but after the fourth or fifth time, something shifted. I started to feel like maybe he cared. I remember one day vividly. I was having an episode, violently vomiting with nothing coming up, and I was completely helpless. He had just stopped by to visit that day. In a panic, he rushed out and called the nurse.

"Come quick, my daughter needs help!"

That moment meant the world to me. I was grateful he was there. I think it might have been the first time I ever saw my father cry. We were both helpless, both scared. The nurse came in and gave me something through my IV to stop the vomiting. My father didn't leave until I fell asleep. Then, to my surprise, he came back the next day.

Despite those visits, not much changed between us afterward. I don't think I saw him again for at least two years.

I often felt like I was the only one of his children who carried such deep emotions about him. But in hindsight, I now realize that some of the best parts of me came from his side of the family. My gentle spirit, my easygoing nature, my dislike for confrontation—all of that came from him. For that, I thank him.

I never understood why I hated arguing or fighting. Growing up, I was teased and called a sucker for not being aggressive like everyone else. It wasn't that I couldn't fight—I just didn't want to. The idea of scratched-up faces and pulled-out hair never made sense to me. That kind of drama was for the birds. My father was the same way. He feared his own shadow, didn't like to argue, and would rather walk away than fight. I get that now.

But I'll never forget the day I found out my father had a set of twins who were the same age as me—and whose birthday was just one day before mine. It crushed me. He called my siblings and me one day and said, "I have three other children I want y'all to meet." We all said okay, thinking nothing of it. He told us he was having a cookout that weekend and planned to bring them along.

Imagine our surprise when he introduced us to three kids. The twins looked to be around my age, and the little girl was a bit younger. After the introductions, we all sat down and talked for a while. When I found out the twins' birthday was the day before mine, my heart sank. I couldn't wait to get home and spill the tea to my mother. I wanted to see her curse him out. My family was messy like that.

I mean, who introduces their legitimate children to their illegitimate children at the age of 16—at a cookout?

The Moment That Impacted My View On Family

That moment changed the way I looked at family forever. I realized then that blood doesn't guarantee trust, honesty, or even loyalty. My idea of what a father was supposed to be shattered that day, and my understanding of family shifted right along with it. I used to think family meant safety—people who were supposed to protect your heart and tell you the truth, even when it was hard. But that day, I felt like a stranger in a group of people I shared DNA with.

I started to question everything—what else hadn't I been told? How many other secrets were hidden behind half-smiles and weekend cookouts?

Instead of feeling whole from meeting more of my siblings, I felt more broken. I didn't blame the twins; they were innocent in all of it. But I was angry at the man who brought us into the world without thinking about how his choices would affect us. I was angry he waited so long to say anything. Sixteen years of silence, and then suddenly he wanted to play happy family.

It made me more guarded. I stopped romanticizing the idea of family. I stopped expecting people—especially men—to show up just because they were supposed to. That day taught me that family isn't about titles; it's about truth, consistency, and presence. If you're not showing up when it matters, what are you really offering?

Still, deep down, I think I was always hoping he'd prove me wrong. I just didn't know how much hope I had left.

From that day forward, I carried a different kind of guard around my heart. I didn't realize it at first, but over time, I saw how it bled into my relationships. I didn't trust people the way I used to—not just men, but people in general. I expected lies. I anticipated disappointment. When someone got too close, I looked for the red flags, even if they weren't there. I kept a backdoor open in every relationship, just in case I needed to leave before they hurt me first.

The idea of vulnerability felt unsafe. How could I let anyone in when the people who were supposed to love me unconditionally couldn't even be honest with me? I started to believe that love always came with betrayal, that the two were somehow tangled together like my own history.

I also struggled with self-worth. If my own father didn't protect me from pain, didn't choose truth over secrets, what did that say about me? It took years to untangle that false narrative—that his shortcomings weren't a reflection of my value. But when you're young and craving affection, consistency, and answers, the silence feels personal. And I internalized that silence. It became part of how I saw myself.

Still, I kept hoping. That little girl in me still wanted to be chosen, to be enough without having to fight for it. And even in all the chaos and brokenness, I never stopped wishing that someday he'd show up, not just physically but emotionally. I needed him to see me, really see me, and to say out loud what he never had: I'm sorry. I should've been there. I should've done better.

But most of all, I needed to forgive him—not for his sake, but for mine.

My father came to live with my family and me about two years before he passed away. He didn't have anywhere else to go, and me being who I am—someone who always tries to do the right thing, even when it's hard—I let him stay with us. Mind you, we didn't really have a relationship. He was more of a familiar stranger than a father. But I opened my home anyway, hoping maybe something would shift.

He stayed with us for about eight months. And to be fair, those months weren't bad. We shared laughs, had small talks, found comfort in daily routines. But our connection wasn't the kind you read about or see in movies. If I'm being completely honest, I treated him more like one of my children than my parent. I looked after him, made sure he ate, kept a roof over his head—things he never really did for me.

When my nephew, who's like a son to me, needed a place to stay, I had to make a hard choice. My father moved out so my nephew could move in. And yes, it was complicated. I know some people might judge me for that, but here's the truth: had he been a present father or showed up for me the way a father should—I would've made room for them both. But the truth is, he hadn't earned that kind of space in my life.

Still, I don't regret opening my door to him. It gave us a chance, however small, to be in each other's lives. It wasn't perfect. It wasn't healing in the way I hoped. But it was something. And maybe, just maybe, that was enough.

Looking back, I'm glad I made the decision to let him stay with us. As uncomfortable and unfamiliar as it felt at times, something in me knew it was the right thing to do. Maybe it wasn't the reconciliation I secretly hoped for, but it was something. A window. A moment. A chance.

Not long after he moved out, I got a phone call that I'll never forget. It was one of those moments that changes the air in the room.

It was an October day—chilly, quiet, uneventful—until my phone rang.

The voice on the other end asked, "Did you know your father is in the hospital?"

I blinked, caught off guard. "No. How would I know that?"

There was a pause. Then, "I heard it's serious this time."

And without thinking, I answered flatly, "Okay... so what do you want me to do?"

"Can you just go check on him?" they asked gently, almost pleading.

In that moment, a flood of emotions hit me—confusion, resentment, guilt, sadness. I wanted to ask, why is it always me? Why was I expected to show up for someone who rarely showed up for me? But something in my spirit stirred. Despite the hurt. Despite the history. Despite the silence that stretched across most of our lives—I went.

Not out of obligation, but out of something deeper. Maybe compassion. Maybe closure. Maybe both.

When I arrived, he was sitting alone in his room, waiting for the doctor. A few minutes later, the doctor walked in and explained that they wanted to perform a biopsy. My father was a long-time smoker, and I braced myself for the possibility of lung cancer. Cancer runs deep on his side of the family—his mother, father, and three of his brothers all passed away from it.

The results were worse than I expected. Not only did he have stage four lung cancer, but he also had pancreatic and bone cancer. On top of that, he suffered from COPD and emphysema.

I was overwhelmed. I didn't know if I cared whether he lived or died until that moment. That moment told me I cared more than I had ever allowed myself to admit.

From that day forward, I decided I was going to be there for him until the end. And I kept that promise. I showed up every single day for thirty days.

It wasn't easy watching him decline, witnessing his pain. He began as an outpatient, but after his first (and only) round of chemotherapy, everything changed. The treatment aggressively attacked the cancer, but it also wreaked havoc on his body. He couldn't finish the full session and had to be hospitalized immediately. Things went downhill fast.

But in those thirty days, something happened. We found closure. We talked for hours each day, asking hard questions and giving honest answers. We cried. We even laughed. And somewhere in those hospital walls, we forgave each other. We healed.

We bonded in thirty days—thirty days. Something we couldn't manage in all the years he was alive and well. All the time we wasted. All the words we never said. But somehow, in those final days, we found each other. We found something real. As the saying goes: better late than never. His last request was simple, but sacred: he didn't want to die in a hospital.

When the doctor told me he had 72 hours left, something inside me shifted. I couldn't let him spend his last breath surrounded by beeping machines and sterile walls. So, I brought him home. I laid him in a space filled with love instead of loneliness.

And twelve hours later—he let go.

But this time, he didn't go alone. He left knowing he was seen, forgiven, loved. And I held his hand, not with bitterness, but with peace.

We didn't get forever. But we got enough to make peace with the past.

REFLECTION

*"Sometimes healing doesn't come in years of closeness, but
in the final days of honesty. We can't rewrite the past,
but we can choose to end the story with peace."*

I worshipped my sister growing up. She was a natural-born artist—she did it all. A seamstress, a hairstylist, a nail tech, a poet, and a nurse without a degree. She had talent flowing through her fingertips and confidence that couldn't be taught. She was popular, had a lot of friends, always had the boyfriends, and could hold her own in a fight. She was one of the "around-the-way girls" everyone respected. I looked up to her. I wanted to be just like her.

But I was the little sister—the tagalong who cramped her style. I wasn't cool enough to roll with her, but I sure tried. I wanted her life. I watched her go to parties and clubs, come home after curfew like it was nothing. And me? I was the one sneaking downstairs to unhook the chain off the front door so she could get in without getting caught.

One night, my mother caught me tiptoeing down the stairs. She looked at me and calmly said, "And if you do, I'm going to beat your ass." That was all I needed to hear. I turned around and walked back up those steps with my head hanging low. I loved my sister, but I wasn't about to get beat for nobody—not even my cool big sister.

After that, my sister came up with a new plan. Genius, really. We took one of her teddy bears, wrapped a headscarf around it, and pulled the covers up to make it look like she was asleep in bed. When our mom did her nightly inspection, everything looked normal. And when she left for work in the morning and took the chain off the door? Safe and sound. I was my sister's keeper.

Even as little girls, her creativity blew me away. She used scraps of our old clothes to design outfits for our Barbie dolls—and let me tell you, **our dolls were fly as hell**. She was vicious with a needle and thread. To this day, she can take an old bed sheet and turn it into a wedding dress. Now that's talent.

When you're young and don't know any better, you fall for everything—especially when it comes to family. I was completely blinded by my love for her. I would do anything to be accepted, to be seen by her, to be loved like I loved her. But eventually, I woke up and realized the truth—that love wasn't mutual. It was one-sided.

I'm not saying I wasn't loved at all—I'm saying my love was unconditional, while theirs came with **conditions**. The moment I started coming into my own, I heard things like, "You've changed," or "You're different now," or "You're mean." And I thought to myself, of course I've changed—you made me this way.

Just because I was the youngest girl didn't mean I deserved to be dumped on over and over again. I gave everything to my family. I went above and beyond, but my support often went unnoticed—until the day I stopped giving it. That's when they noticed.

People will go out of their way to destroy you, even when they know you don't deserve it. It's the hate inside them that keeps them going. But me? I could never hurt someone on purpose. And if I did, I'd be the first to apologize—even when I wasn't at fault—just to keep the peace.

I'm not the vindictive type. I don't waste my energy on foolishness. I don't run around telling everyone who will listen when something goes wrong—I sit with it, I hold it inside, and I let it be. What's done is done. You can't take it back, but you can make sure it doesn't happen again.

It took me 47 long years to get to that place—to truly let it be.

If you're not a positive influence in my life, you won't be a part of my life. No exceptions. Family, friend, or stranger—I've made peace with protecting my peace.

I'll say it: I secretly hated my sister. Maybe it was the way I admired her for so long, only to realize that admiration wasn't mutual. Maybe it was the way her love always came with strings. Or maybe it was because I loved her unconditionally, but she loved me on terms I didn't understand. Either way, I started choosing me, and with that came peace.

Then there's my younger brother. Let's just say... he has a gift for B.S. (laughs). He can talk his way into—or out of—just about any situation. From the moment he opens his mouth, you know it's probably nonsense, but he sells it with such confidence that you find yourself considering it anyway. He could sell you the shirt off your own back if you're not careful.

Growing up, he got on my last nerve. He was always joking, always clowning. But no matter what he did, I couldn't stay mad at him for long. I'd be in the kitchen cooking and he'd be all good—until I was done. Then he'd walk up, stick his finger in my food and say, "You still want that?" knowing full well I'd toss the whole sandwich in the trash. I'd be furious, but that was him. Always doing something to get a reaction.

And then there's my baby brother—my wild child, my mystery. He was a natural-born hustler. From a young age, he had a soft spot for animals. He'd go to the creek and come back with a frog, a lizard, a turtle, or something squirming in his pocket. When he wasn't at the creek, he was wandering the alleys bringing home stray cats and dogs.

He was different from most boys in the neighborhood. He wasn't into sports. He liked cooking, fast cars, motorcycles, fishing, boxing, older women, and money. But the thing that stood out most was his attitude. My baby brother had a temper like no other. He was angry—deeply angry—and I saw that anger harden into something darker over the years. So much bitterness in one heart. His energy was so volatile that I used to dread late-night phone calls, afraid that one day I'd get that call that he was either gone or locked up.

Unfortunately, I received both of those dreaded calls—one telling me my brother was in jail, and years later, another saying he might not make it out alive. At different points in his life, I watched him face some of the darkest moments anyone could endure. My brother did a 10-year bid, and it was during that time behind bars that he began his transformation. In prison, he tapped into his hidden talents. He earned his High School Diploma, got certified in every program available, and even taught himself to speak two foreign languages fluently.

People often wondered why my baby brother was so protective of me. Why he stood up for me like his life depended on it. The answer is simple; I protected him first.

I was his shield before he ever had the strength to lift one for himself. I was there when the world wasn't kind to him—when he was beaten, cursed at, or had his hard-earned money snatched away after cutting grass or hauling people's trash just to make a few dollars. I saw the way life tried to harden him before he even had the chance to dream.

I held him during the darkest moments—rocking him while he cried, wiping his tears as he asked me with a broken voice, "Why do bad things always happen to me?" And I never had the answer. All I had were my arms around him, my love for him, and a quiet promise that I'd never let him face the pain alone.

That bond—built in pain, held together by love—is something death could never erase. He's gone now, and not a day goes by that I don't feel the weight of his absence. But when I think of how fiercely he loved me, how he guarded me with everything he had—I remember it was because I did the same for him first.

We were each other's safe place in a world that didn't always feel safe.nAnd though he's no longer here, the memory of that love still protects me.

I was there when he brought turtles, lizards, fish, stray dogs—any animal he thought he could save—into the house. I helped him hide them. I helped him scavenge through the trash to find places for them to sleep. We found everything from shoeboxes to milk jugs, old fish tanks to soda bottles. His love for animals ran deep, and fishing was another thing that brought him peace.

I'll never forget the first time we went fishing together. He got the hook stuck in his hand. You'd think that would have made him hate fishing but no. My uncle pulled the hook out, patched him up, and my brother loved fishing even more after that.

We had dreams together. We were planning to go into business—me with an event planning company and a laundromat, him with a consignment shop full of gently used designer clothes and a bakery. He was serious about entrepreneurship. Every morning, we would meet to brainstorm. It was the first time I ever heard of a business plan.

These are the things people didn't know or understand about us. My baby brother taught me a lot.

I've come to realize that being born into a family doesn't automatically make you family. Blood may connect us, but true family is built—it's nurtured through love, trust, support, and effort. Yes, I have siblings, but I don't have any sisters or brothers. Once upon a time, I had both. Now, the heartbreak of broken relationships sits heavy on my heart.

Over time, I've learned that family can be chosen. I've met strangers who have been kinder, more uplifting, and more consistent than some of the people I share DNA with. It's a painful truth to admit—that I have so many relatives, yet I often feel completely alone. I've always been the supportive one, the dependable one. The one who showed up—every time, no questions asked.

Need a ride? Call Tiny.

Need food? Call Tiny.

Need a place to stay? Call Tiny.

Need a job or resume? Call Tiny.

But one day I sat still long enough to ask myself: Can I count on everyone the way they count on me? Sadly, the answer was **no**. I can count on one hand the people I can truly depend on—and most of them aren't related to me.

Jealousy isn't always about material things. People can have all the money, status, and possessions in the world and still envy you. Why? Because you work hard and play harder. Because your light shines naturally while theirs dim under the weight of bitterness. Because you have a winning personality, and they carry an attitude. Because you know how to make things happen for yourself—and that threatens them.

I grind every day. Sometimes I juggle two or three jobs on top of being a full-time wife and mother. And yet, all some people choose to see are my vacations—four a year. What they miss is that I earned every single one. I'm not just working to survive. I'm working and living at the same time.

And now? I've learned to be done. Not mad. Not bitter. Just done.

But here's the truth: when you stop putting everyone else's needs before your own—when you start saying no, stop picking up the phone, stop overextending yourself—people will say, "You've changed."

And they're right. I **have** changed. Because you can't grow, evolve, or move forward by staying the same. What people don't understand is that this change didn't happen overnight. It wasn't a simple switch—it was a battle. One I fought within myself for years. I wrestled with guilt, fear, and doubt. But at some point, I had to make a decision: either keep self-destructing or start protecting my peace.

I chose peace.

I was physically and emotionally drained, trying to be everything to everyone. My life felt heavy and out of control. Change wasn't optional, it was necessary.

Letting Go of Family Ties

Letting go of people who share your blood is one of the most painful decisions you'll ever have to make, but sometimes, it's the most necessary one.

My older sister walked away from me without looking back. And I, in turn, had to sever ties with my middle sister before she died. That still haunts me—not because I regret protecting myself, but because I never imagined our story would end that way.

I also severed ties with my younger brother. And with all of my siblings on my father's side—those relationships were buried with him. He was the glue. Flawed, yes. But still the binding force that held us together. When he passed, the connection we once had dissolved faster than the sound of his last breath.

I've always had a good heart. I've always tried to be the bigger person. I gave more chances than I should have. Extended grace where there was none given to me. Bent until my soul ached. Because I was taught to believe that family is everything.

"Blood is thicker than water," they said. And I held onto that like gospel. I believed it meant we'd always choose each other. That no matter what, family would stand—even if everything else fell apart.

But I was wrong.

The most devastating wounds I carry weren't inflicted by enemies—they came from people I called family. And the hardest truth I've had to face is this: just because someone shares your blood doesn't mean they know how to love you. It doesn't mean they value you. It doesn't mean they're meant to stay in your life.

Letting go of them wasn't an act of hate. It was an act of self-preservation. A final attempt to save what was left of me.

I didn't walk away out of anger. I walked away out of exhaustion. After years of trying, forgiving, explaining, and hoping. After realizing that no matter how much love I gave, it would never be enough to heal what they refused to acknowledge.

And when I severed those ties, it felt like amputating parts of myself. Like tearing down a house I helped build.

The grief didn't show up all at once. It came in moments. In quiet holidays. In missed phone calls that will never come. In memories that feel more like old wounds than warm stories.

There are still days when I wonder what could have been. If we had tried harder. If we had chosen humility over pride. If love had been louder. If I had more time with my sister before she was gone for good.

But I've learned something that changed me forever: you don't owe anyone the pieces of yourself they keep breaking. Not even family.

I love them in my own way. I probably always will. But I love myself more now. Enough to walk away from what hurts. Enough to protect my peace, even if it means walking this path alone.

And that... that's what real healing looks like.

JOURNAL ENTRY

I Believed It Because My Heart Needed To

Not every memory with my family was dark. Not every moment with my siblings was laced in pain or chaos.

Sometimes, I felt loved—even if it was a front. I believed it because that's what my heart needed. It needed something to hold onto in the middle of all the mess.

I remember one night clear as day: my sister fixing me a plate before she made her own. It wasn't much—just fried chicken, a scoop of rice, and a biscuit—but it felt like everything. She slid it toward me and said, "Here, I saved you the bigger piece." For a few fleeting minutes, I wasn't invisible. I wasn't just the baby sister trying to keep up. I was seen.

Moments like that became my lifeline. A laugh shared in the kitchen. A secret whispered under the covers. A hand grabbing mine during a storm. Maybe it was temporary. Maybe it wasn't genuine. But in those moments, I felt chosen. And when you're starving for connection, even crumbs of love can feel like a feast.

I know now that love isn't supposed to come with conditions or confusion. It's not supposed to hurt or make you question your worth. But back then, I took what I could get. Because broken love still feels warm when you've been living cold.

This doesn't mean I excuse the hurt or pretend the trauma didn't happen. It did. But I also don't want to erase the moments that gave me hope, even if they were fleeting. Because in a world where I often felt invisible, those glimpses of love—real or not—helped me survive.

My love, commitment, and support were always real from the beginning. Even now, I still love them all. I just love myself more.

So no, life with my family wasn't all bad. It was layered. It was complicated. It was survival dressed in sibling laughter and a mother's "I love you" that didn't always feel real, but still meant everything to the little girl in me who desperately needed to hear it.

And today, I hold space for both truths: the pain and the love. Because acknowledging both is how I finally started to heal.

Interlude

YOU DON'T KNOW ME

*Y*ou don't know me.

Because if you did, you would know that what happens between us stays between us.

If you knew me, you would know that our disagreement has nothing to do with our children—they are innocent, and I will never use them as pawns.

If you knew me, you would know that I don't run my mouth to every ear that will listen.

What happens between you and me is not for the world—it's for us to work out, not to perform for an audience.

If you knew me, you would know that when I do something for you, it's from my heart, not for credit, not for clout, and not for anyone else's approval.

If you knew me, you would know that I am slow to anger and quick to apologize—even when I'm not wrong—because peace matters more to me than pride.

If you knew me, you would know that yes, I've changed—because how could I not? Growth hurts, but staying the same would've killed me. I refuse to shrink just to make you comfortable.

If you knew me, you would know that just because my mother, my sister, my brother, or anyone else is mad at you—that has nothing to do with me. I don't pick sides. I stand on integrity.

If you knew me, you would know that my family is off-limits. You don't have to like me, but you will respect my boundaries.

If you knew me, you would know that I'm approachable. If you think I said or did something wrong, you can come to me. I'll set your mind at ease right then and there—no guessing, no gossip, no games.

If you knew me, you would know that I am uniquely and wonderfully made. I don't need to compete with you, and I could never want to be you—I am too busy being the best version of me.

And if you really knew me, you would know this: I don't think I'm better than anyone—that's your thought, not mine. I'm too busy figuring out how to enhance my own life to compare it to yours. I am my only competition. I can cheer for you, support you, and celebrate you without losing a single night of sleep—because your success doesn't threaten mine.

If you knew me, you would know that I want to see you win. I would rather help build you up to your face than tear you down behind your back.

If you knew me, you would know that I value resolution over revenge, love over grudges, and growth over gossip.

But the truth is, you don't know me.

And that's okay—because everything I just said? I live it whether you see it or not.

Growth will make people think you've changed on them, when in reality, you've just changed for you. The version of me you used to know tolerated things that disrespected my peace. She swallowed her words to keep other people comfortable. She stayed quiet while others lied on her name. But that version of me is gone.

I've learned that integrity has a cost—you lose people who can't handle accountability.

Boundaries have a cost—you lose people who only liked you when you were easy to use.

And growth has a cost—you lose people who are committed to misunderstanding you.

But I wouldn't trade this new version of me for anything. Because even when it hurts, even when I stand alone, I stand free.

Growth hurts... But staying broken would've hurt more.

So no, you don't know me. But one day, when growth comes for you too, you'll understand exactly why I had to change.

CLOSING PRAYER

God,

Family is where I've known both my deepest wounds and my greatest love.

Some bonds built me up. Others broke me. But through it all, You were there.

Teach me to forgive what still hurts, honor what remains, and release what no longer serves my healing.

Help me build a family rooted in truth, grace, and Your unshakable love.

Restore what can be mended, and give me peace with what cannot.

In Jesus' name,
Amen

Chapter 10

◇◇◇

HEALING THE HEART

◇◇◇◇◇◇◇◇◇◇◇

"Healing the heart isn't about forgetting the hurt – It's about remembering you were worthy of love the whole time."

◇◇◇◇◇◇◇◇◇◇◇

etting go of who others thought I was—and standing firm in who I knew I was becoming—set the stage for the next battle: healing my own heart. Because integrity isn't just about how you treat others. It's about how you treat yourself. And for years, I abandoned my own heart while trying to hold everyone else together.

Chapter 10 is the part of my story where I finally turned inward— where the healing that I had been chasing in other people had to begin with me.

I was stuck in this vicious cycle for so long that I almost didn't make it out. I was in denial about everything, or maybe I just didn't want to accept my truth. When what you lived is the only thing that you've ever known, learning and accepting a new truth had a detrimental effect on my health. I was literally sick during my healing process.

Healing didn't come from time alone—it came when I finally surrendered. When I stopped trying to carry the weight of it all on my own. When I fell to my knees and cried out to God, desperate for a healing that I couldn't create by myself. I asked God to help me do what I couldn't do alone: to forgive the ones who hurt me. To forgive myself for the times I stayed too long, loved too hard, or lost pieces of myself trying to be enough.

I fasted.

I prayed.

I poured out every broken part of me at His feet.

And in that surrender, something miraculous happened: God met me there—right in the middle of my wreckage. He didn't ask me to have it all together. He just asked me to be willing. Piece by piece, prayer by prayer, tear by tear, God began to heal the places in me that I thought would stay broken forever.

I realized that forgiveness wasn't about excusing what was done. It was about setting myself free from the chains of bitterness, resentment, and regret. It was about trusting that God would take my pain and turn it into something beautiful—something holy.

Forgiving them was hard. Forgiving myself was even harder. But God was patient with me, showing me that I was never alone, not even in the moments when the world made me feel abandoned.

Healing my heart wasn't a quick process—it was a sacred one. It was the beginning of a new relationship with myself, with my past, and most importantly, with my Creator.

This healing was different. It wasn't survival. It was resurrection.

Once God began to heal my heart, I realized something even deeper—I wasn't just meant to survive. I was meant to live.

For so long, my dreams had been buried under layers of pain and disappointment. I had stopped believing that real joy, real peace, and real love were possible for me. But God gently pulled me out of that grave.

He reminded me that I was still His daughter, still chosen, still loved, still destined for more than brokenness.

As I reconnected with God, I started dreaming again. I started hoping again. I started believing that the promises spoken over my life weren't dead—they were simply waiting for the right season to bloom.

I no longer carried shame for the time it took me to get here. Healing isn't a straight line. It's messy. It's painful. But it's worth it.

Each time I chose forgiveness over bitterness, I loosened another chain. Each time I chose love over fear, I unlocked another door. Each time I chose faith over despair, I planted another seed of life.

I realized that healing isn't forgetting—

It's remembering without reliving.

It's loving from a distance when necessary.

It's honoring your growth, even when others can't see it.

I stopped begging for validation from people who could never give it. I stopped waiting for apologies that were never coming. I gave myself permission to move forward, carrying only what would help me, not what would haunt me.

Healing the heart takes courage. It takes surrender. It takes grace—endless, abundant grace—both from God and for yourself.

And slowly, surely, I found my way back to me. Not the broken version. Not the silenced version. But the redeemed, restored, unapologetically free version.

The woman who chose to rise.

The woman who dared to heal.

The woman who finally understood that she was never too lost for God to find.

I am not the same woman who once begged for love, who once cried herself to sleep wondering if she was enough. I am the woman who stood in the ashes of her pain, raised her hands to heaven, and declared, *I will not die here.*

Healing didn't erase the past—it redeemed it. And with every scar, every tear, every prayer whispered through trembling lips, I built a new legacy. A legacy of freedom. A legacy of faith. A legacy of fierce, unbreakable love beginning with myself.

The heart that once ached now beats with purpose. The soul that once wept now sings with hope.

I am healed.

I am whole.

And by the grace of God, I am finally free.

Finding myself wasn't some big, dramatic moment. It happened little by little—in the quiet, in the stillness, in the moments where I finally got tired of pretending I was okay. I started peeling back the layers, not just of pain, but of patterns.

I began asking the hard questions: Why did I allow this? Why did I stay? Why did I feel like I needed to prove myself to people who were supposed to love me unconditionally?

The truth hit hard, but it also freed me: I wasn't broken; I was bruised. There's a difference. Broken implies I needed fixing. Bruised meant I needed healing.

I stopped trying to be who everyone else expected me to be and started becoming who I was always meant to be.

I reclaimed my voice—the one I'd silenced for years out of fear of rejection or being labeled "too emotional," "too much," or "too sensitive." I stopped shrinking myself to fit into the spaces where I was never meant to be comfortable.

Healing didn't mean I forgot the past. It meant I stopped letting it define me. I used to carry every insult, every betrayal, every unkind word like they were part of my identity. Not anymore. Now I carry peace. Now I carry power. Now I carry purpose.

I'm not angry. I'm awake.

I'm not bitter. I'm better.

And I'm no longer waiting for people to give me what I've already given myself: validation, love, and the freedom to be fully, unapologetically me.

REFLECTION

For so long, I thought love meant sacrifice—giving all of me, even when there was nothing left. I thought loyalty meant staying, even when I was hurting. I thought being "good" meant being silent, agreeable, and available. But I've learned that true love includes boundaries. True loyalty includes mutual respect. And being "good" should never come at the cost of your own peace.

I used to feel guilty for choosing myself. Now I feel grounded.

I used to second-guess my worth based on how others treated me. Now I know that how people treat me is a reflection of them, not me.

I've walked through some dark seasons where silence was louder than words and loneliness felt heavier than heartbreak. But in that stillness, I met me. Not the version shaped by trauma, not the version constantly proving her value—but the real, raw, honest me. And I like her. I'm proud of her.

Healing isn't just about letting go of the past—it's about reclaiming your future. It's about no longer waiting for permission to be free.

This version of me doesn't beg to be chosen. She chooses herself.

She knows her worth.

She protects her peace.

She walks away when needed.

And she smiles—not because life is perfect, but because she's finally at peace with who she is becoming.

CLOSING PRAYER

God,

My heart has been through battles it never asked for. It's held grief, betrayal, anger, and the ache of unanswered prayers. But I'm done patching it up with temporary fixes. I give it fully to You—every scar, every crack, every guarded corner. Heal what the world wounded. Restore what trauma tried to steal. Make my heart whole again in Your love.

In Jesus' name,
Amen

Chapter 11

LOVE & MARRIAGE

◇◇◇◇◇◇◇◇◇◇

"I stopped chasing love that made me disappear.
Now I know love should build, not break. And the
first heart I had to honor... was my own."

◇◇◇◇◇◇◇◇◇◇

Honey, before we start on this chapter, let me inhale and exhale. Some people are fortunate enough to find their life partner early on. Others, like me, have had to figure it out through hard lessons and lived experiences. Nothing has ever come easy in my life, but I wouldn't change a single thing. Every experience—good, bad, and heartbreaking—has shaped me into the phenomenal woman I am today.

I'm not even sure I've ever truly been in love. After my first love broke me, I vowed never to love or be faithful again. My relationships with men were complicated. I carried abandonment from my father and neglect from my mother, even if they didn't see it that way at the time.

My first official boyfriend... here we go, back down memory lane. It was the late '80s. I was about 14 or 15—light brown skin, long hair, and a body grown women envied. I remember walking home when this older-looking guy tried to talk to me. I thought he was grown—maybe thirty! I ignored him. But a few days later, I saw him in our school lunch line. Turns out, he was a student and just two years older than me. From then on, he walked me home every day, carried my books, and slowly broke down my tomboy wall. I eventually gave him a chance, and surprisingly, he was one of the kindest boys I had ever met. A true gentleman. I made the decision to be intimate with him—a decision I planned out on my own. Looking back, I wish someone had guided me. That's why I always say: Ladies, talk to your daughters. Don't sugarcoat it. Tell them what to expect.

Then there was my first love. November 1988. Lord, love makes you do some dumb stuff. I was obsessed. So much so, I nearly dropped out of high school trying to keep up with him. If it wasn't for my cheer coach stepping in, I would have. She gave me the wake-up call I needed. I ended up doing day, night, and summer school to graduate on time. Meanwhile, he was tangled up with every girl around the way, and I was just happy to be the "main." I cringe now, but back then, that title meant something to me. After that relationship ended, I vowed to never be faithful again. He had broken me. That pure heart I had? Gone.

After him, I tried to make every man "the one." The one to listen to me, love me, support me, be faithful, communicate, and cherish me. I didn't know how to receive love anymore. I was either guarded, emotionally unavailable, or just going through the motions.

I've been married four times—twice to the same man. I was 21 the first time, and I never even had the chance to live on my own or truly know myself. If I could do it over, I would have traveled, learned to love myself deeply, discovered my worth, and embraced life on my terms.

My first husband was one of my baby brother's good friends. He was kind. He was steady. He was mature in all the ways I wasn't ready to be. He treated me with a gentleness I didn't know how to receive.

And I broke his heart.

Not because he wasn't good to me—but because I was still chasing chaos.

Still chasing the highs and dysfunction I had grown addicted to. I thought I wanted peace, but the truth is... I didn't know what to do with it. So when he walked away—when he gave up on trying to hold together a woman who didn't know how to stay still—I let him go. And I ran straight into the arms of destruction.

My second husband wasn't love—he was lust.

To be honest, it started as nothing more than a booty call. The sex was incredible, and I let that be enough. That's how he got me—with pleasure, not purpose. I confused chemistry with compatibility. I mistook passion for love. He wasn't emotionally safe. He was a liar, a gambler, a cheater. And when he couldn't manipulate me with charm, he used his fists.

Back then, I was so desperate to feel something that I let sex blind me to the truth. I told myself I could fix him, that maybe love would be enough to change him. But all I ended up doing was losing myself. At one point, both men—yes, both—proposed to me within a day of each other. One offered me safety. The other offered chaos dressed as desire. And in my brokenness, I accepted both. It was messy, selfish, confused, and a clear reflection of how lost I truly was inside.

Eventually, I chose my daughter's father. I remarried him, hoping we could rewrite our story. But jealousy and broken trust tore us apart. We couldn't rebuild something that had never truly healed. And when that fell apart, I went back. Back to the second man. Back to the fire I already knew would burn me. We got married, and that marriage lasted three toxic years. Three years of lies. Three years of pretending. Three years of slowly losing parts of myself I couldn't get back.

But eventually, I left. And I didn't go back.

Even now, when I think about those years, I feel the weight of regret—not just for the men I chose, but for the woman I was when I chose them. Lost. Insecure. Desperate for love, even if it came wrapped in pain. That woman didn't know her worth. She didn't know that love wasn't supposed to hurt. She didn't know that sex could never fix a bleeding soul.

I carry the lessons now, not with shame but with understanding. Because that part of my story—as broken, complicated, and messy as it was—made me the woman I am today. Wiser. Stronger. And finally done choosing pain over peace.

Then came my now-husband. We met at a seafood cookout in 2004. When I saw him, my exact words were, "Damn." I was thirty-one and assumed he was younger, but turns out we were the same age. We exchanged numbers, started talking, and clicked instantly. But then he disappeared. I thought he ghosted me, so I deleted his number. Turns out, he had been shot and was in ICU. When he called me to explain, I didn't believe him and hung up. It took my sister begging me to visit him in the hospital before I finally went. He didn't even know I was there, but once he found out, he called me. We talked every night after that. And we've been together ever since.

Seventeen years strong, but not without our challenges. Every relationship, every heartbreak, every lesson brought me to him. My husband is my safe space, my peace, my partner in everything. He saw the best in me when I couldn't see it myself. He took my flaws and still stayed.

It hasn't been easy with my husband. We had a power struggle. I would preach that a spouse should come first in marriage, but I didn't practice it. I always put family before him. I was wrong. You can replace a man, sure. But if you keep doing that, you'll never build something lasting.

My husband deserves a lifetime of appreciation. I knew how to attract a man, but I didn't always know how to be a good partner. He stayed because he saw something in me I hadn't yet discovered.

Now, after all I've been through, I love myself deeply. I know what it means to be honest, loyal, and whole. I've grown into a woman who values peace over chaos, love over lust, and partnership over possession.

Yes, I've been married four times. No shame in my journey. Every step led me here—to a marriage I cherish, to a man who held on when I didn't know how, and most importantly, to myself.

REFLECTION

Love has never been a straight road for me. It's been a winding path filled with lessons, heartbreak, laughter, and healing. Every failed relationship, every wrong turn, and every hard goodbye taught me something valuable. I used to think love meant losing yourself in someone else. Now I know love starts with knowing who you are and what you deserve.

I'm no longer chasing fairy tales or trying to fix broken people to feel whole. I've lived, I've learned, and I've grown. And through it all, I've discovered that real love—the kind that lasts—is rooted in truth, grace, and self-respect. I may not have had the perfect start, but I've *Finally Figured It Out.*

CLOSING PRAYER

God,

Love hasn't always been safe—or simple. I've loved through fear, fought through pain, and learned how to rebuild from ruins. Thank You for restoring what I once believed was unworthy of love. And God... for the men I hurt along the way—whether in my brokenness, my confusion, or my silence—I lift them up to You.

Heal what I could not. Restore what I unknowingly damaged. I release guilt and shame, and I ask for Your mercy to cover them too. Teach me how to love with wisdom, to receive love with grace, and to build with someone who reflects Your heart. Bless my marriage. Let it be a sacred space for truth, safety, and joy.

In Jesus' name,
Amen

Chapter 12

ILLNESS & HEALTH (MY BODY, MY BATTLE)

⬦⬦⬦⬦⬦⬦⬦⬦

*"This body has been through hell. But it's
still mine. Still breathing. Still rising.
And now? I honor it—not for how it looks, but for how it lived."*

⬦⬦⬦⬦⬦⬦⬦⬦

I've struggled with my weight for most of my adult life. After years
of therapy, I came face-to-face with the truth: I was an emotional
eater.

When life hurt—when I felt abandoned, broken, or overwhelmed—I didn't cry, scream, or shut down. I ate. Food became my
comfort, my coping mechanism, my silent friend. I didn't just snack—I
binged. I numbed myself with every bite.

And then the pandemic hit. Isolation locked us all in. I wasn't just
emotionally overwhelmed—I was physically still. No distractions. No
escapes. Just me, my thoughts, and the kitchen. This time, it wasn't

emotional eating. It was survival eating. Boredom eating. Routine eating. And I gained weight. A lot of it.

But here's the truth I need the world to understand: I never had a problem with my weight. Other people did. And maybe they still do. But that's their burden, not mine. Whether I drop twenty pounds or keep every single one, my joy isn't up for negotiation. I'm not chasing society's definition of beautiful. I'm not seeking validation from a scale or a stranger. I'll walk it off or I won't. Either way, I'm still showing up in full love and honor of the woman I am.

Because peace begins when you stop performing for the world and start living for your reflection. And me? I've finally arrived at that place—where confidence is louder than criticism and self-love outweighs every judgment.

My Feet, My Fight

Back in 2009, I was jogging every day around the Suitland High School track. My feet were on fire, but I kept pushing. I wanted to prove something to myself, to the world. After every run, the pain got worse. I could barely walk, but I still laced up those shoes.

Eventually, I saw a podiatrist. Plantar fasciitis. It sounded like a made-up word. But the pain was real—sharp, stabbing, and un-relenting. I had two options: surgery or cortisone shots. I chose the shots.

Every three months, they stuck long, burning needles into both feet. I clenched my teeth and gripped the exam table until I went numb. The relief came fast, but it never lasted. Eventually, the pain came back with vengeance. I couldn't walk across a room without flinching. Couldn't stand in a grocery line without sweating.

And then came the moment that shattered me: a routine fire drill at work. Everyone else calmly filed out. I stood frozen at the top of the stairs—paralyzed by pain. I had to be rolled away in an office chair, like a patient. Like a burden.

That moment broke me. If it had been a real fire, I wouldn't have made it.

That's when I scheduled the surgery. I started with my left foot—the one that screamed the loudest with every step. The recovery time was supposed to be 90 days. But I went back to work in just six weeks. Why? Because I was afraid. Afraid of losing my job. Afraid of being seen as replaceable. I didn't fully understand what medical leave really meant or that I had rights. I pushed my body back into the grind too soon, and I paid for it. My body wasn't ready and it let me know in no uncertain terms.

When it came time for my second foot surgery, I did it differently. This time, I listened. I honored the full 90-day recovery. I gave my body what it deserved: rest, stillness, and healing.

Eight months after my first surgery, I stood—really stood—on my own two feet. No pain. No limp. Just strength and grace. It was like walking on a promise fulfilled.

That surgery—those tears, those long nights—turned out to be one of the best decisions I ever made.

Vegas, Vision, And A Diagnosis That Changed Everything

In 2016, my husband and I took a trip to Las Vegas. We had barely been there two days when something in my body felt... off.

At first, it was subtle—annoying, but manageable. I was running to the bathroom every five minutes. I couldn't stop drinking water, cranberry juice, and Gatorade like my life depended on it. But no matter how much I drank, I couldn't quench the thirst. It felt like I was drying out from the inside.

By the third day, my body was giving out. My energy disappeared.

My head was spinning. Every sip made me feel worse. I tried to rest, hoping I'd bounce back, but my body had already crossed a line I couldn't see.

When it was time to head home, I couldn't even walk through the airport. My legs felt like sandbags. My vision blurred. I could barely whisper. I looked at my husband and said, "Call the EMTs. Now."

They arrived quickly and tested my blood sugar. It was so high, their machine couldn't even register it. At the hospital, the numbers told a story I didn't want to hear: A1C: 13.5. Blood sugar: over 900

The doctor didn't sugarcoat it: "If you had boarded that plane, you would've gone into a diabetic coma mid-flight."

That moment shattered everything. My health. My illusions. My sense of control. I wasn't just sick; I was in crisis. And I knew then life would never be the same.

I was hospitalized for a full week. After discharge, I had no health insurance, no primary care physician, no plan. But I was referred to a free clinic, and that clinic became one of the greatest blessings in my life. They took me in, no judgment. No red tape. Just care.

The Weight Of It All

I didn't have weight loss surgery to be skinny—I did it to live.

The goal was to reverse the diabetes, not erase my identity. I dropped almost 100 pounds. I went from 274 down to 180, and from size 20 to size 10.

Everyone cheered. "You look amazing!" they said.

But I didn't feel amazing. I felt like a ghost in my own skin. All my life, I was the thicker one. That was who I was. And now, I was a stranger. I hated being small. I missed me.

The only person I told the truth to was my husband. He looked at me one day and said, "You look unhappy."

"I am," I said.

That conversation saved me. I made a choice: I started gaining some weight back. Slowly. Intentionally. Not to throw away my progress—but to reclaim my peace. I gained 40 pounds back. Landed at a size 14. That's my happy place. That's where I feel beautiful again.

It's been almost seven years now. My diabetes is undetectable. My glucose stays under 6. Glory be to God.

A Testimony Of Survival: What Tried To Take Me Out Only Brought Me Closer To God

Before the surgeries, before the diagnosis, before the life I live now—back in the year 2000—I faced one of the greatest battles of my life.

It came out of nowhere. Like a storm I never saw coming.

I had just started working at a pathology office when my body began to betray me. The office felt like a freezer, but inside I was burning up. My temperature was 102. I told myself it was just a cold. I went home, hoping to sleep it off. But by morning, the chills were worse, my muscles ached like I'd been hit by a truck, and the fever had only climbed higher.

Still… I went to work. Still… I pushed through. Because that's what I had always done.

That was my first mistake.

That morning, on the highway, I blacked out behind the wheel. Gone. Just like that. I don't remember how I got to safety. What I do remember is waking up in a haze of flashing lights, voices yelling, hands pulling me out of the car. My husband at the time was with me in the vehicle. God sent someone to take the wheel that day. That's the only explanation. Because by all accounts, I shouldn't have made it.

At the hospital, my temperature had skyrocketed to 104.2. They ran every test. They pumped me with medication. Then they moved me into isolation—hazmat suits, masks, gloves. No one could touch me. I felt like a danger. Like a burden. Like a ghost. And worst of all—no one had answers.

The virus moved fast. First my eyes, then my entire body. Each day I grew weaker.

Then came the memory loss. And finally... paralysis. The entire right side of my body shut down. I couldn't walk. I couldn't write. I couldn't hold a fork. I couldn't even hold myself together.

I spent a full month in that hospital fighting for my life without a name for what was killing me.

After I was discharged, I finally got the call: West Nile Virus. But by then, the damage was done. The virus stole three years from me. A year and a half of paralysis. A lifetime of lessons. And the worst part? It didn't just rob me. It robbed my daughter, too.

She was still just a child. But life didn't let her stay one. While her friends were playing and laughing, she was at home—cooking, cleaning, taking care of me. She mothered her mother. She carried the weight of survival on her small shoulders. And she never once said, "Why me?"

That guilt—that deep ache—never fully leaves. But so does the honor. Because the real hero of that season wasn't me. It was her.

To this day, doctors still can't explain why the virus hit me so hard. But I know why. Because sometimes God allows what we don't understand to break us open—to prepare us for something greater. What was meant to destroy me became the very thing that anchored me in faith. His power was made perfect in my weakness.

I wasn't just healed. I was transformed.

The Fog Years

My memory between 2000 and 2020 was mostly a blur—compliments of the West Nile virus. I only remembered fragments of my past, like puzzle pieces scattered in a box with no lid. It wasn't until 2020 that those pieces slowly started to come back together. I'm still not sure if I had blocked things out as a form of protection or if my mind was simply too cluttered and overwhelmed to recall anything clearly.

The pandemic gave me plenty of time to sit with my thoughts. In those quiet, reflective moments, something strange began to happen—I started remembering. At first, it felt like déjà vu. I kept seeing myself as a toddler, jumping out of my crib.

Then came another flash: trying to pull my baby brother out from under the kitchen table. He was fat as hell, and no matter how hard I tried, I couldn't get him out. That was his favorite hiding spot.

Before the virus, my mind was razor-sharp. I could glance at a 16-digit number once and never forget it. My brain was a vault. After the virus, everything changed. I had to start writing everything down. The frustration of forgetting was unbearable. One minute, I felt like Rain Man. The next, I felt like Radio. That swing between brilliance and brokenness was its own kind of torment.

Sometimes I wonder if losing those years was a gift or a curse. Because in the silence of forgetting, I finally started to remember who I really was.

REFLECTION

I once thought survival meant pretending I wasn't in pain. But survival is what my body already knew how to do—it fought, even when I wanted to give up. Healing, though—that was a choice. I had to learn to rest when I wanted to run, to nurture what I had once ignored, and to thank God for the vessel that carried me through fire. My scars remind me that brokenness isn't the end of the story. This body isn't my enemy. It's my witness.

CLOSING PRAYER

God,

My heart has been through battles it never asked for. It's held grief, betrayal, anger, and the ache of unanswered prayers. But I'm done patching it up with temporary fixes.

I give it fully to You—every scar, every crack, every guarded corner. Heal what the world wounded. Restore what trauma tried to steal. Make my heart whole again in Your love.

In Jesus' name,
Amen

Chapter 13

WHEN RELIGION HURTS, BUT GOD HEALS

◇◇◇◇◇◇◇◇◇◇

"Religion didn't save me—relationship did. And the God I know now? He sees me, loves me, and walks with me. No performance required."

◇◇◇◇◇◇◇◇◇◇

Religion And Routine

"Come to me, all you who are weary and burdened, and I will give you rest... For my yoke is easy and my burden is light," Matthew 11:28–30 (NIV)

I'm not religious—I'm spiritual. There's a difference, and it took me years of heartache, confusion, and soul-searching to figure it out.

As children, people often assume we don't understand what's happening around us. But we do. We see it. We feel it. And I saw too much, too soon.

Church was supposed to be a safe place. My grandmother raised us in the church, and I believed her when she said the sanctuary was where broken people found healing. But the reality was different. Sunday mornings were less about grace and more about rules. Dress right. Act right. Speak right. Don't ask questions.

I remember the white tights, the patent leather shoes, the heavy hush that fell the moment we walked through the doors. I can still hear the choir belting out hymns that rattled the wooden pews. I'd sit swinging my legs, waiting for the moment when all that singing would make me feel something. Waiting for a love that matched the words. But more often than not, I walked away emptier than I came.

The Hurt Beneath The Hymns

Religion quickly became performance. People played church like it was theater. The deacons with booming voices, the deaconesses with their sharp tongues, the secretaries who smiled on Sundays and gossiped on Mondays. They were loud about holiness but quiet about kindness.

I'll never forget walking into the women's bathroom one Sunday. I was just a girl, but I had ears. They didn't care that I was standing there while they tore into each other like schoolgirls. Their whispers were daggers, their laughter cutting deeper than the sermons we'd just heard. I stood frozen, wondering how the same mouths that sang "Amazing Grace" could drip poison so easily.

They used fear like a leash. "You going to bust hell wide open," they'd say, wagging fingers, as if hellfire was their favorite scripture. And in my head, I whispered, "Right after you." I wasn't being disrespectful—I was just trying to make sense of a God who was supposed to be love, but was constantly being weaponized to shame me into submission.

A Wounded Faith

It's devastating when the people you're told to trust turn out to be frauds. The place that was supposed to nurture you ends up wounding you. Adults swept everything under the rug, but rugs only collect dirt. Eventually, it spills out, and when it does, it shakes the faith of those who once believed without question.

Looking back, I see how fear dictated my choices. I got married at 21—not because I was ready, but because my pastor said sex before marriage was sin. I wanted the guilt to stop, so I rushed into a covenant I didn't understand. I thought I was saving my soul, but what I was really doing was sacrificing my truth.

Religion bound me with shame. God, I later realized, wanted me free.

Meeting God Outside The Walls

It wasn't until I reached the end of myself—broken, empty, and out of options—that God stepped in. Not when I was polished. Not when I had it all together. But when I was crumbling from the inside out.

One night I sat in my car after leaving a service. I had sung the songs, clapped at the right times, smiled through the motions. But the second I shut the door, I broke. I sobbed until I couldn't breathe. My Bible sat in the passenger seat, and I remember whispering, "God, are You even real? Because if this is all You are… I don't want it." And in that moment, I felt Him. Not the God of rules. Not the God of fear. But a God who met me in my tears like a warm blanket wrapped around my shivering soul.

That's when it clicked: religion hadn't saved me. Relationship had.

The Pivot

God didn't wait for me to show up at the altar. He met me in the wreckage. He didn't ask me to be perfect. He just asked me to be real.

Religion said, "Hide your scars." God said, "Show them—I'll heal them."

Religion said, "Perform." God said, "Be still."

Religion said, "Earn it." God said, "Receive it."

And when I finally surrendered, healing began. Not because I followed the rules, but because I let Him in.

REFLECTION

I used to think God lived in four walls, behind pulpits and pews, and that if I got the ritual right, I'd be safe. But God found me in the places religion never reached—in my doubt, in my questions, in my silence. What religion couldn't give me, His presence supplied: grace without condition, love without performance, and truth without shame. My faith is no longer borrowed from tradition. It's built on relationship.

CLOSING PRAYER

God,

I was wounded where I was told I'd be healed. I was judged when I needed grace. Silenced when I needed to be seen. But in the spaces where religion failed me—You never did.

Thank You for meeting me outside the walls, for speaking when others wouldn't listen, and for loving me past doctrine and image. Heal the spiritual wounds I carry. Separate Your truth from their traditions. Teach me to walk in relationship, not just ritual. And may I never confuse Your heart with the hurt they caused.

In Jesus' name,
Amen

Chapter 14

LIVING IN FREEDOM

◇◇◇◇◇◇◇◇◇◇

"Freedom isn't just the absence of chains—
it's the presence of peace."

◇◇◇◇◇◇◇◇◇◇

Freedom isn't just the absence of chains—it's the presence of peace. It's waking up and no longer feeling the weight of old wounds dictating my day. It's making choices not out of fear, but out of love, especially love for myself. Living in freedom means I no longer apologize for the space I take up. I no longer shrink, bend, or twist myself into something more acceptable. I am enough exactly as I am, without explanation and without compromise.

Freedom means boundaries without guilt. It means love without conditions. It means joy that isn't borrowed or dependent on anyone else. Living in freedom is trusting my voice, my instincts, my journey. It's forgiving myself for the years I didn't know better—and celebrating the woman who fought her way through the darkness to find the light.

I honor the lessons, but I refuse to relive the pain. I carry the memories, but I refuse to carry the shame. I live—fully, bravely, unapologetically. This is the life I fought for. This is the life I deserve. And this is the life I am proud to claim, one breath, one step, one victory at a time.

If you take nothing else from my story, take this: mental illness and behavioral health are very real. People suffer in silence because they fear the unknown. They're afraid their voice won't matter, afraid they won't be believed. Be mindful of the people around you. You never know the impact your presence, your words, or even your silence might have on someone who's quietly watching—someone who's hurting.

I am a living example of both—someone who has suffered in silence and someone who kept pushing, even when I felt like I had nothing left. Many will be mad at me simply because they don't understand my truth. But please don't be mad. Don't be offended. Instead, sit with it. Think about the role you may have played in my story.

I take ownership of everything I've ever done—the good, the bad, and the downright ugly. I've never claimed to be perfect, and I never will. We all have a past. The difference now is that I refuse to let mine keep me bound. If I keep letting people drag me back into who I used to be, I'll never become who I was meant to be. I can't change the past. I can't control the future. All I have is the present, and every single day I choose to grow, to evolve, and to become a better version of me.

They may have held my past—but God holds my future.

I'm not just free for me. I'm free for every woman who thought she had to suffer in silence. My freedom is my testimony. And I'm finally living it out.

REFLECTION

Freedom isn't loud—it's steady. It's waking up without apology, choosing peace over people-pleasing, and creating space for joy in a world that tried to drown it. I've learned that freedom isn't something the world hands you; it's something you claim. It's the courage to stop living for who you were, and to step fully into who you're becoming. This freedom is my revolution, and I will protect it with everything in me.

CLOSING PRAYER

God,

For so long I didn't know what freedom felt like. I was bound by shame, guilt, fear, and the lies I believed about myself. But You stepped in and broke the chains—one truth at a time.

Thank You for reminding me that freedom isn't earned, it's received. I don't have to be perfect. I don't have to have it all figured out. I just have to trust You… and walk. Help me protect the freedom You gave me. May I never shrink to fit back into the boxes You've broken me out of.

I am no longer a prisoner to my past—because whom the Son sets free is free indeed.

In Jesus' name,
Amen

Freedom Manifesto

I am no longer bound by what broke me.
I have faced the ashes of my past and refused to be buried there.
I cried, I bled, I screamed in the silence – but I did not quit. I rose.

Breaking the Chains

I am no longer available for anything or anyone who dishonors my
spirit. I no longer shrink myself to be accepted.
I no longer betray myself just to belong.

Healing the Heart

I forgive, not because they asked – but because my soul demanded it.
I release the chains of bitterness, the prisons of resentment,
the illusion that their choices define my worth.
They don't.
God does.

Living in freedom

I was not created just to survive; I was created to overcome.
I was created for joy. for wholeness, for freedom.
Today, I honor the woman I've fought to become:
Unshaken. Unbroken – Unapologetic
I carry the scars, but they are not signs of defeat – they are proof
that hell couldn't have me.

Final Chapter

SHATTERING GENERATIONAL CURSES: THE FINAL BREAKTHROUGH

◇◇◇◇◇◇◇◇◇◇

"I held the weight my family never spoke of and broke it in silence so future generations could finally breathe."

◇◇◇◇◇◇◇◇◇◇

I spent so many years trying to fit in, never realizing I was born to stand out. One morning, at the age of forty-nine, I sat up in bed with tears streaming down my face. Not the heavy, hopeless tears of the past, but tears that felt like release. For the first time in my life, I whispered to myself, *Enough.* Enough of living on autopilot. Enough of building everyone else's vision while neglecting my own. Enough of shrinking just to be accepted.

That morning, I looked in the mirror and saw a woman I barely recognized—not because she was broken, but because she was free.

After all the trauma, drama, life lessons, and healing, I finally figured it out: I'm not meant to blend in. I'm meant to shine. I stopped hiding behind the opinions of others and embraced the gift of being uniquely me.

I've learned how to be the love of my own life, how to wear my crown without needing someone else to hold it straight. I've learned how to say no without apology, how to choose battles that matter and let go of the ones that don't, how to pour into myself the way I used to pour into everyone else. And the greatest discovery? My worth was never lost—I just had to claim it.

The Anthem Of My Becoming

For years I sabotaged my own progress—afraid of change, afraid of failing, afraid of finally being seen. But fear doesn't get the last word anymore. I turned the pain into a passport, and it carried me into freedom. I turned the shame into soil, and it grew into wisdom. I turned the curses into dust, and I built something new from the rubble.

One of my proudest titles will always be "mother." Not just mom, but nurturer, healer, chauffeur, counselor, and protector. No paycheck in the world compares to the purpose I've found in raising my children. But the truth is, my healing had to happen for their sake, too. Because what I don't deal with, they inherit. And I refuse to hand them chains when I was called to hand them wings.

Freedom Requires Release

God has gently—and sometimes forcefully—removed people, habits, and mindsets that once kept me stuck. I used to cling to people out of fear: fear of being alone, fear of starting over, fear of who I'd be if I finally put myself first. But freedom requires release. You cannot rise while holding hands with what's pulling you under. So, I closed doors. Some slammed shut, others I locked quietly and walked away. Each one was necessary. Each one cleared space for the life God had waiting for me.

Now, I don't need everyone to understand me. I just need to stay aligned with the One who created me. And in that alignment, I've found a version of myself I actually like—whole, healing, and finally free.

Forgiveness And Full Circles

Before I close this chapter, I have to say this:

To those who hurt me—I forgive you. Maybe you didn't know the depth of your words. Maybe you didn't realize your actions would leave scars I'd carry for years. Maybe you did. Either way, I'm done carrying it.

And to those I've hurt—I'm sorry. From the deepest place in me, I'm sorry. For the sharp words, the broken promises, the walls I built instead of bridges. I hope you find peace, the same way I finally have.

Forgiveness doesn't excuse what happened—it releases what still lingers. And in releasing you, I've released me.

My Charge to You

As I write these words, my tears aren't from sadness—they're from gratitude. I made it. I lived. I healed. I grew. And now I'm here, handing this truth to you:

You can shatter every chain, every curse, every compulsion. You can reclaim your life. You can rise from the very things that were meant to bury you.

I am proof. Not polished proof, but living proof—scarred, tear-stained, still learning proof. And if I could figure it out, so can you.

This isn't the end of my story. It's the beginning of a new one—one written in purpose, peace, and legacy.

Now it's your turn. To rise. To break. To shine.

CLOSING PRAYER

God,

I didn't just survive the storm—I walked out carrying the victory. What was meant to silence me only made me louder in truth. What was passed down to break me became the very thing You used to build me.

Thank You for trusting me with the weight of transformation. For every curse I shattered, every tear I cried, and every scar I carry—thank You for the redemption hidden inside.

Cover my children. Cover their children. Let the freedom You gave me flow through every branch of my bloodline. May the healing never stop with me—but begin because of me.

The chains are broken. The silence is over. The story is redeemed. I give You the glory. I walk in the breakthrough.

In Jesus' name,
Amen

JOURNAL ENTRY

I Believed It Because My Heart Needed To

Not every memory with my family was dark.

Not every moment with my siblings was laced in pain or chaos.

Sometimes, I felt loved, even if it was a front. I believed it because that's what my heart needed.

It needed something to hold onto in the middle of all the mess. A laugh. A hug. A shared secret. A plate fixed just for me. Little things that made me feel like I mattered. Maybe it was temporary. Maybe it wasn't genuine. But in those moments, I felt seen.

I know now that love isn't supposed to come with conditions or confusion. It's not supposed to hurt or make you question your worth. But back then, I took what I could get. I accepted crumbs and called it a feast because even broken love still feels warm when you're starving for connection.

This doesn't mean I excuse the hurt or pretend the trauma didn't happen. It did.

But I also don't want to erase the moments that gave me hope, even if they were fleeting.

Because in a world where I often felt invisible, those glimpses of love—real or not—helped me survive.

My love, commitment, and support were always real from the beginning. Even now, I still love them all. I just love myself more.

So no, life with my family wasn't all bad.

It was layered.

It was complicated.

It was survival dressed in sibling laughter and a mother's "I love you" that didn't always feel real, but still meant everything to the little girl in me who desperately needed to hear it.

And today, I hold space for both truths: the pain and the love.

Because acknowledging both is how I finally started to heal.

The Journey Continues

*P*icture this: the woman who once lived bound by silence now stands tall, hands open, face lifted toward the light. No chains at her feet. No shame weighing down her shoulders. Just peace. Just presence. Just purpose. That's me.

This isn't the end.

Finally Figured It Out was about survival. About breaking generational curses, finding my voice, facing my truth, and learning to love myself through it all.

But healing isn't a final destination—it's a lifelong journey.

The pain didn't disappear overnight. The storms didn't magically stop. But something inside me shifted. I stopped surviving and started becoming.

Now, I'm walking differently.

Now, I'm living with intention.

Now, I'm standing in my purpose—

not just figuring it out, but living it out. Which is why this story doesn't stop here.

The next chapter of my life deserves its own space. Its own fire. Its own voice.

Finally Free: From Surviving to Standing in Purpose is the continuation of my journey—the part where I stop explaining my scars and start showing how I built something beautiful from the broken pieces.

If you've ever wondered what happens after survival… keep turning the page. Because the best is yet to come.

Anthem Line

"Survival was my beginning. Purpose is my becoming."

Reader Charge

And as you close this chapter, let me leave you with this: Don't stop at survival. Don't settle for silence. Don't believe the lie that your scars disqualify you. They don't. They're proof you're still here.

So rise. Shatter every chain. Reclaim your life. Live in the freedom you fought for. Because if I figured it out, you can too.

And if I'm free… so are you.

PART II

Finally Free

From Surviving to Standing in Purpose
(A continuation of Finally Figured It Out)

Introduction

I remember the first morning I woke up and realized survival wasn't
enough anymore. The sun felt different. My breath felt lighter.
Something inside me whispered, "Now, you live." That was the moment I knew my story wasn't ending—it was only just beginning.

If you've read the first part of my memoir, *Finally Figured It Out:
Shattering Generational Curses*, then you already know the weight of the
battles I've fought—and the freedom I found when I finally stopped
surviving and chose to heal. But healing doesn't end with a revelation. It continues with a decision. A decision to walk out what you've
learned, to practice what you've prayed for, to build a life that reflects
the woman you've become.

That's why I wrote this second part.

This is not just the continuation of my story; it's the evidence of
what happens when you dare to live in the purpose God has placed on
your life. It's about the messy middle between brokenness and breakthrough, the sacred process of becoming whole, and the quiet courage
it takes to start again with intention.

I'm speaking directly to you—the woman who's tired of performing, the one who's forgiven everyone but herself, the one who feels too
far gone or too ashamed to begin again. I see you. Because I was you.
And by the grace of God, I'm becoming her now—the version of me I
once thought I'd never reach.

This book is for every soul who has ever felt the weight of

dysfunction, the silence of separation, the ache of self-discovery. It's for the daughters who became mothers while still healing their inner child. It's for the women who kept going, even when no one clapped. It's for the ones who chose peace over people-pleasing, purpose over performance.

Thank you for walking this part of the journey with me. Thank you for being ready—not just to figure it out, but to finally live it out. Because this isn't just my story anymore—it's our blueprint for freedom.

With love,
Rhonda Harris

"So if the Son sets you free, you will be free indeed."
—John 8:36 (NIV)

Affirmation

I am no longer bound by who I was.
I am walking fully in who I am becoming.
My freedom is not fragile—it is secured by God.
After years of surviving, breaking generational cycles,
and piecing myself back together, I stepped into a new
season. One marked by purpose, intention, and peace.
This next part of my journey isn't about the fight to survive.
It's about the freedom to live.
To live boldly.
To live healed.
To live as the woman I was always becoming.
This is no longer just the story of what I overcame.
It's the story of how I chose to truly live.

Chapter 1

THE WOMAN IN THE MIRROR

◇◇◇◇◇◇◇◇◇◇

The old me had to die so that the healed me could rise

◇◇◇◇◇◇◇◇◇◇

There were days I couldn't even look at myself. Not in the mirror. Not in pictures. Not even in passing reflections. It wasn't just shame—it was disconnect. I didn't recognize the woman staring back at me. Her eyes looked tired. Her face wore the weight of battles no one else saw. Her smile didn't reach her soul.

She looked like me… but she didn't feel like me.

Because for a long time, I was just a version of who life made me. Shaped by trauma. Hardened by survival. Held together by prayers I didn't always believe and strength I didn't even know I had. I wasn't living; I was enduring. I was exhausted. And yet, somehow, I kept going.

But God.

God never stopped pursuing the real me, even when I forgot who she was. He met me in my brokenness, not with judgment, but with grace. He whispered my name when all I could hear was shame. And slowly, day by day, He began to reintroduce me to myself. Not the woman shaped by wounds, but the woman shaped by purpose.

That was the beginning of my transformation—not a makeover, not a glow-up, but a resurrection. The old me had to die so that the healed me could rise. And that healing didn't come from the world. It came from knowing who I am in Him.

Now, when I stand in front of the mirror, I don't flinch. I look at myself and I see every storm I've outlasted. I see every battle I've won in silence. I see every time I could've broken down but got back up. I see the scars, but they don't define me anymore. They remind me—that I survived. That I was chosen. That I was never alone.

I see a woman who has been through hell and made it holy. A woman who used to be hard just to feel safe but now chooses peace. A woman who doesn't shrink anymore. Who doesn't perform anymore. Who walks in rooms with presence, not for applause, but because she knows God walks with her.

There was a time when I only saw what was missing. Now I see what was restored. I see beauty in my boundaries. I see strength in my softness. I see power in my voice. I see a woman who no longer needs permission to exist fully, loudly, and unapologetically.

And the most beautiful part? I didn't just find her. I fought for her. I prayed for her. I became her. Because God reminded me of who I've always been.

I no longer fear the mirror. I meet it with honor. Because the woman I see now? She's not perfect, but she's real. She's not without pain, but she's free. She's not who she used to be, but she's finally who she was always meant to be.

CLOSING PRAYER

God,

For years I couldn't look at myself without shame. I only saw the pain, the mistakes, the woman shaped by survival. But You never turned away. You saw me when I couldn't see myself. You called me beautiful when I called myself broken. Today, when I stand in front of the mirror, I see what You see: a daughter, a survivor, a woman becoming whole. Help me to never forget that my reflection is proof of Your redemption.

In Jesus' name,
Amen

Chapter 2

PEACE THAT I FOUGHT FOR

Worth Every Battle Scar

I used to mistake chaos for normal. Silence made me anxious. Calm made me suspicious. If the phone wasn't ringing, someone wasn't arguing, or something wasn't falling apart, I'd assume something was wrong. I didn't know how to rest. I didn't know how to just be.

For most of my life, conflict wasn't the exception—it was the expectation. It lived in my house growing up, walked with me into relationships, sat next to me at work, and followed me into motherhood. I didn't start fights for no reason, but I didn't walk away from them either. I was always ready for war, even when no one declared it.

But after a while, always being "on guard" stops feeling like strength. It starts feeling like prison. And at some point, I got tired. Tired of waking up with tension in my chest. Tired of always having the last word. Tired of replaying arguments in my head just to feel justified. Tired of living in survival mode even when I wasn't under attack. That's when I realized: I wasn't addicted to drama… I was just unfamiliar with peace.

Peace didn't come easy. I didn't wake up one day and suddenly feel still. I had to fight for it. I had to unlearn everything I thought made me strong. I had to stop reacting to every comment, every slight, every bit of disrespect. I had to let people be wrong about me and still choose calm. I had to walk away from conversations that would've once pulled me under. I had to forgive people who didn't even ask.

And most of all—I had to forgive myself. Because sometimes the war wasn't with the world. It was with me. With the version of me that thought love had to be loud. That thought being guarded was the same as being wise. That thought peace was a luxury for people who had easier lives. But God taught me something different.

He showed me that peace isn't a luxury—it's a promise. It's not something the world can give or take away. It's something He deposits in your soul when you surrender the need to control everything. Peace isn't quiet because nothing is happening. Peace is quiet because you trust God to handle what's happening.

Now peace looks like choosing not to argue just because I can. It looks like soft music in the background while I cook. It looks like deep breathing instead of deep sighs. It looks like protecting my home, not just from strangers, but from energy I don't want to live with anymore.

Peace looks like me saying "no" without guilt. It looks like shutting my phone off when my spirit says rest. It looks like worship music on a Monday, like prayer at the kitchen sink, like journaling my thoughts before they explode. It looks like me, finally, living like I'm not at war anymore.

I fought hard for this peace. And I'll fight just as hard to protect it. Because I know what it cost me to get here. And I know how easily the world will try to pull me back into chaos. But I don't live there anymore.

I live in peace. I speak from peace. I lead with peace. Because I've seen what happens when I don't. And I've felt the joy that comes when I do.

This peace? It's mine. God gave it. And I'm not giving it back.

Interlude

---◆◇◆---

I DIDN'T JUST BREAK THE CURSE—I REBUILT MYSELF

They said breaking the curse was enough—but they didn't see the wreckage it left behind. I didn't just break it. I bled through it. I cried through it. I clawed my way through every shattered piece of myself. And when the dust finally settled, I didn't recognize the woman staring back at me. She was bruised, but not broken. Fragile, but not weak. She carried the softness I was once shamed for and the strength I had to fight to reclaim. I realized then: healing wasn't about becoming who I used to be. It was about becoming who I was always meant to be.

There was a time I thought strength meant survival—keeping my guard up, swallowing my emotions, and always pushing through. But I've come to learn that real strength is being able to feel and still move forward. It's crying and continuing. It's saying "no" and not explaining. It's choosing yourself without apology.

For years, I believed I had to be hard to be respected. That softness was weakness. That gentleness would get me hurt. But I was wrong. My softness is sacred. It took more courage to let down my walls than it ever did to build them. It took more faith to speak kindly to myself than to keep rehearsing pain. I stopped shrinking to fit what others expected and started expanding into who I truly am.

The truth is, I didn't just walk away from the generational curses—I had to mourn what they cost me. The childhood I missed. The relationships I ruined trying to earn love. The version of me that was so desperate for approval, she lost herself in the process.

But here I stand—rebuilt. Not polished or perfect. Not without scars. But whole. And this time, the foundation isn't fear, survival, or trauma. It's self-worth. It's grace. It's knowing that I am enough even when I rest. Even when I say no. Even when I am not everything for everyone.

I rebuilt myself with truth. With boundaries. With softness. With God. And the woman I am now… she's not afraid to let the light in.

Chapter 3

---◈◇◈---

THE POWER IN MY NO

Not Everything Deserves Access to Me

For too long, I said "yes" when my spirit was screaming "no." Yes to people who drained me. Yes to opportunities that weren't mine. Yes to staying silent when I should've spoken up. Yes to being what everyone else needed—even when it cost me.

I used to think saying "yes" was the kind thing. The Christian thing. The strong thing. But really, it was the exhausted thing. The fearful thing. The people-pleasing thing. And I carried that habit like a badge of honor—available to everyone, loyal to a fault, putting myself last and calling it humility.

But God had to teach me: saying "yes" to everything isn't obedience. Sometimes it's disobedience, because I was agreeing to things He never told me to carry.

I remember one moment in particular when everything shifted. Someone I had always bent over backward for asked me for something they had no right to expect. In the past, I would've given in. I would've made room at my table, even if it meant pushing myself into the corner.

But this time, I said no. Not out of spite. Not out of anger. But out of love for myself.

And I'll never forget the feeling afterward. Not guilt. Not shame. Peace.

When I started saying "no," I started breathing again. I stopped answering the phone for chaos. Stopped showing up out of guilt. Stopped pretending to be okay with being overlooked, underappreciated, or used. I stopped letting people violate my boundaries and then blame me for bleeding.

Saying "no" is holy. It's how I honored my time, my energy, my calling. It's how I made room for rest, for healing, for purpose. It's how I finally stopped living my life on everyone else's terms and started living on God's.

Because His voice is often quiet. And you can't hear Him clearly if you're too busy responding to everything else.

Now, I say "no" without guilt. No to what doesn't serve my peace. No to what disrupts my home. No to people who only come with crisis. No to spiritual manipulation that makes me feel like setting boundaries is sin. No to anything that tries to drag me back into the version of myself I've already outgrown.

And you know what I've learned? Every "no" to them… is a "yes" to me. To my healing. To my purpose. To my assignment. To my family. To my God.

I am no longer afraid of being misunderstood. I am no longer shrinking to stay liked. I am no longer exhausted from being everything to everybody. I don't owe anyone access to me just because they remember who I used to be.

This version of me? She is intentional. She is guarded by grace. She is led by peace. And she is not afraid to say no.

CLOSING PRAYER

God,

Teach me to say no without guilt and yes without fear. Help me discern what's meant for me and give me the courage to walk away from what isn't. Show me that protecting my peace is not a punishment to others—it's obedience to You. Strengthen me to stand firm in truth, and remind me that boundaries are a reflection of love—starting with love for myself.

In Jesus' name,
Amen

THE APOLOGY I NEVER GOT (BUT FORGAVE ANYWAY)

*D*ear You,

I waited years—decades, really—for two small words: I'm sorry. I pictured them falling from your lips like gentle rain, imagined their sound swelling in the quiet places you left inside me. I was certain that if you finally named what you did—the silence, the abandonment, the careless bruises I carried in secret—my shattered heart would knit itself whole.

But the apology never came.

So, for a long time I sat in the ache of its absence. I measured my worth against your refusal to own the harm. I tried to outrun the memory of slammed doors, the sting of words spoken in anger, the nights I lay awake replaying moments that stole my innocence. Every unchecked wound turned into armor—sharp edges meant to protect me, but they cut the people who tried to love me next.

Then one lonely sunrise, I heard a whisper in my spirit: forgive anyway.

Not because you earned it. Not because you sought it. But because my freedom was never meant to hinge on your remorse.

So, I wrote this letter.

I forgive you for the promises you dangled like stars and let burn out when dawn came.

I forgive you for the fists you called discipline and the words you called truth.

I forgive you for the years I spent believing love had to hurt before it could heal.

I forgive you for telling me who I was not—unworthy, too much, never enough—and for every time I swallowed that lie as gospel.

I forgive you for the shadow you cast over my reflection, for the way I learned to shrink so I wouldn't trip over your insecurity.

I forgive you for the apology you will never give.

I release it—like a dove from trembling hands—back to the sky where only grace can reach it. I am done rehearsing courtroom speeches in my mind, done standing on the witness stand begging the jury of your conscience to deliberate. The verdict is in: I was always worthy, always lovable, always meant to rise.

Forgiveness does not rewrite history, but it does hand me the pen. From this day forward, I get to choose how the story ends. I choose peace over poison, growth over grudges, healing over hardness. I choose to bless you on your way and bless myself on mine.

If ever you find the courage to say those words—I'm sorry—know that they will land softly on ground already made holy by my letting go. But if that day never comes, my heart will still be light, my steps still steady, my soul still free.

Because forgiveness was never a gift I owed you; it was the ransom I paid to set me free.

With grace and unshakable peace.

~Rhonda Harris

Chapter 4

<hr/>

MY DAUGHTER, MY REFLECTION

How Our Bond Has Evolved and What I've Learned from Her Resilience

There's a certain kind of ache that comes when you see yourself in your child, especially the parts you had to fight so hard to heal.

From the moment she was born, she became mine. I inherited her the day she entered this world, and I raised her from day one. I held her, fed her, protected her, and loved her as if my heart had given her life. Because in every way that matters, she is my daughter.

For a long time, I didn't realize that I had passed down more than just my laughter and lessons. I had also unknowingly passed down pain—the trauma, the survival patterns, the unspoken dysfunction I had carried for far too long. I thought I had shielded her from it.

But pain has a way of seeping into the cracks we don't even know are there.

When my daughter started dating, I watched closely. I paid attention to every sign, her moods, her reactions. I asked the hard questions. I didn't want her to follow my path, but sadly, she lived what she learned.

A few years ago, she walked away from all of it— from the noise, the chaos, the dysfunction. At first, I didn't understand. I was heartbroken. I cried myself to sleep more nights than I can count, convinced I had lost her for good. I replayed every moment, every word, every silence, trying to figure out where I went wrong.

But in the middle of my grief, something began to shift. God started to show me what I couldn't see through my pain. She did what I couldn't do—she walked away.

She left to find her healing. To find herself. And in that separation, I began to understand the depth of her pain—the weight she had carried, the courage it took to set it down.

I started to pray for her in a different way. Not for her to come back, but for her to find peace. To find her happy place. And somehow, in the process, I was inspired to find mine.

I see now that God had to separate us for a time. Not to break us apart, but to break us open. To stretch us. To heal us. To make us into what He created us to be—together.

Now, our bond is different. Deeper. We speak with more honesty, more grace, more respect. She's not just my daughter—she's my teacher, my mirror, my reminder that breaking the cycle is not only possible, it's necessary.

She chose herself. She chose her child. She chose peace. And in doing so, she gave me permission to do the same.

She is my reflection—not just of who I was, but of who I'm becoming. Not just of the struggle, but of the strength. Not just of the pain, but of the power.

I thank God for her—for the way she loves, the way she fights, and the way she walked away when staying would've been easier. Because of her, I now know that sometimes distance is a door God uses to lead us both home.

With love, humility, and gratitude.

Chapter 5

PARENTING GROWN CHILDREN

Releasing Control, Choosing Guidance Over Correction

No one prepared me for this part.

They told me about sleepless nights with newborns, the chaos of toddler tantrums, the backtalk that would come with adolescence. But no one warned me that one of the hardest parts of motherhood would be learning to let go—not just of their hands, but of my need to fix, to shield, to steer.

Parenting grown children feels like holding a mirror to your own journey—your wins, your wounds, your wishes. I see myself in them, sometimes in ways I'm proud of, other times in ways that humble me to my knees. And still, I love them fiercely.

But the struggle? It's real.

You raise them with prayers and sacrifices, hoping they'll make better choices, avoid your mistakes. You want so badly to say, "I've lived this. I know how this ends. Just trust me." But grown children don't always want advice—sometimes, they just want space. And learning to love from that space takes a level of surrender I wasn't ready for.

I have a grown daughter. A grown son. And a 10-year-old I'm still raising. Three very different hearts, three very different seasons, and one mama still trying to get it right. I'm still learning how to guide without controlling, how to be present without being overbearing, how to offer wisdom without forcing direction.

Every day, I'm trying to be a better version of myself for them—to be an example of what it looks like to grow with grace, to love without strings, and to admit when I'm still figuring it out.

I remember the day my daughter gave birth to her daughter. My baby girl—this little girl I once rocked to sleep, who used to fall into my arms when life got too loud—was now bringing life into the world herself. I stood in that delivery room both proud and terrified. Proud of her strength. Terrified by how real the letting go felt.

Watching her hold her baby for the first time was the moment it hit me like a wave: she's not just my daughter anymore. She's someone's mother. Her own woman. Her own story.

And in that moment, I whispered a quiet prayer: God, help me let go.

It wasn't about walking away—it was about stepping back. It was about trusting that everything I had poured into her, every lesson, every prayer, every late-night talk was enough. That God would do the rest. And He has.

My oldest son is a work in progress. Quiet, steady, hard to read. He's so much like his father—nonchalant, calm, almost distant at times. For years, I couldn't tell if he was soaking in life's lessons or letting them pass him by. I used to worry, used to wonder if anything I said ever stuck. He never gave much reaction, never asked many questions, never showed much emotion.

But in time, I learned something humbling: he was always listening. Always watching. Always understanding in his own way. He just moves in silence; a gift it took me my entire life to learn.

Now I see pieces of wisdom he tucked away showing up in how he carries himself. In his choices. In the quiet strength behind his eyes. I don't always hear from him, but when I do, I hear myself in his voice. Not the loud, dramatic parts—but the thoughtful ones. The grounded ones. He is growing into a man in his own time, on his own terms. And I've learned to respect that.

Then there's my youngest. The one I didn't see coming. I wasn't ready for him—but I had no idea how much he would stretch and grow me. From the moment he was born, he did everything on his own time. He still does. You can't rush him, push him, or persuade him against what he knows to be true in his heart. He's decisive, strong-willed, and incredibly aware. He questions everything, challenges anything that doesn't sit right in his spirit—even me.

And yet, he has a heart of gold. He loves hard and deep. He's all about family, so much so that it sometimes scares me. The way he holds on, the way he feels everything, the way he cares—it's powerful, almost overwhelming. But it reminds me that love can be both fierce and tender at the same time.

With him, I'm still in the thick of parenting. Still in the trenches of everyday teaching, learning, and letting go. He reminds me to be present. To listen more. To slow down and trust that even the youngest among us carry wisdom that can shift generations.

I've said things I wish I hadn't. Tried to control what wasn't mine to carry. Offered correction when what they needed was compassion. And still, they come to me. Maybe not always with open arms, but with hearts that are trying, learning, growing—just like mine once did.

There are days I grieve the versions of them that needed me more. The little hands reaching for mine. The calls that came just to say, "I love you." I miss that simplicity. But I'm also learning to embrace who they're becoming, not just who they were.

This chapter of parenting requires patience, prayer, and a quiet kind of strength. It's not about having all the answers. It's about becoming a safe place they want to return to. A place where they're not judged by their stumbles but loved through them.

Sometimes, I bite my tongue until it bleeds. Sometimes, I cry after the conversations that don't go well. But every day, I try again. Because I'm not just their parent—I'm their lifelong anchor. And even anchors need to learn how to loosen their grip so the ship can find its own way.

I'm still learning. Still growing. Still loving them from near and far, with every ounce of grace God gives me, I realize something powerful:

Letting go doesn't mean giving up. It means trusting that what you've poured into them—your love, your lessons, your legacy—is enough to carry them through.

And when it's not, I'll still be here. Always.

With love and surrender.

REFLECTION

Leading Them Out of the Nest

You can't push your children out of the nest. You have to lead them out.

Some kids just aren't ready for the outside world—not because they're incapable, but because home feels too safe. Too familiar. Too much like the womb. And honestly, as mothers, we just know. We can sense when they're not ready, even when the world is shouting, "It's time."

When I was growing up, things were different. I was ready to leave the nest early—not because I was prepared, but because life didn't give me a choice. Survival pushed me out before I could even stretch my wings. But today's world is different. Our children are growing up in the comfort we prayed for, in the stability we never had. And in giving them everything we lacked, we unintentionally made them dependent on us, on comfort, on the idea that they never have to struggle.

Sometimes being there as their crutch makes them lazy. They grow content. Comfortable. In today's society, they've adapted to quick fixes—picking up odd jobs like rideshare or food delivery, making just enough to support their habits or desires, and then crawling right back into their safety zones. It's not that they're incapable of more—it's that no one has truly challenged them to rise higher.

We have to teach them that living like that is temporary. That survival isn't the same as living. We don't just want them to get by—we want them to thrive. To build something real. To know the satisfaction of working toward something bigger than their next impulse.

We want what's best for them. But they have to want it, too.

Depending on someone else to carry you through life is a sure way to fall. Eventually, the support will stop showing up. And if they haven't learned how to stand on their own two feet by then, the fall could break them.

That's why we can't just push them—we have to prepare them.

We equip them with life's necessary tools. Financial wisdom. Emotional strength. Boundaries. Resilience. And then, when the time is right—whether they feel ready or not—we let them go. We cut the rope, but not before they've learned how to climb. Yes, they might fall at first. That's part of it. But I can be at peace with the fall if I know in my heart that I did my best to prepare them for the climb.

Because one day, they will leave the nest. And when they do, I don't want them just surviving—I want to see them soaring.

Chapter 6

WHEN I REACHED BACK FOR MY BROTHER

How Obedience to God Led to
Family Reconnection

Some stories of healing don't start with a breakthrough—they start with silence. With separation. With wounds that don't bleed on the outside but run deep through the heart.

This one is different. It's not a story of betrayal, but of misunderstanding. Of guilt misplaced. Of someone I loved, pushed away, and eventually—by the grace of God—welcomed back in.

When my father died, I severed ties with almost everyone on his side of the family. There was too much drama, too many unresolved tensions, too many wounds reopened every time I tried to stay connected. The dysfunction exhausted me, and I decided to walk away—for my peace, for my sanity, for my healing.

But in the process of protecting myself, I made one devastating mistake: I shut the door on my brother. He wasn't part of the mess. He had never stirred the drama. He had always stayed neutral—never choosing sides, never speaking ill, always showing up when I needed him. But I made him guilty by association.

And for eleven years, I treated him like the rest—like someone who had betrayed me. When in truth, he had done nothing but love me.

Through the years, he reached out. He sent messages, extended grace, checked in from time to time. But I didn't have the space to receive it. My walls were too high. My pain too thick. I wasn't ready.

But God has a way of softening even the hardest places.

During my journey—somewhere between breaking generational curses and finding peace—I felt a nudge. Not loud, not forceful. Just a quiet whisper from God saying, *Reach back.*

So I did. At first, I was still guarded. Still distant. Still unsure. But he didn't flinch. He didn't hold it against me. He didn't make me beg. He just loved me.

And then came the moment that changed everything. We reconnected at my older sister's funeral service. I saw him sitting there, shoulders shaking, sobbing uncontrollably. Grief had broken him open. And something inside me—something I thought had hardened—moved.

Without thinking, I walked over and sat next to him. No words. Just presence. I reached for his hand and held it, gently. As if to say, *I'm here. I never stopped caring.* He leaned into me, still crying, and I found myself silently praying, *God, help us both heal.*

That moment reminded me of something I had forgotten: love never really dies—it just gets buried beneath the pain.

As time passed, we spoke more. Laughed again. Let our guards down. And eventually, I realized I owed him an apology—not just for the silence, but for placing him in a category he never belonged to. For turning away from someone who had only ever tried to love me well.

God led me to that moment. And when it came, I didn't hesitate. I apologized. I told him the truth. I invited him back into my life—not out of obligation, but out of genuine love. It was something we had both longed for, even if we never said it aloud.

Today, we are reconnected in a mighty way. Our bond is stronger. Our conversations are deeper. Our love is rooted in forgiveness and gratitude.

I thank God every day that he never gave up on me. I thank God that love waited.

Because sometimes, obedience looks like reaching back. And sometimes, reconciliation comes not through confrontation—but through humility, grace, and time.

I'm so grateful he gave me both.

CLOSING PRAYER

God,

Thank You for restoring what was nearly lost. Thank You for grace that reaches across silence, time, and pain. I pray You continue to bless the bond between me and my brother. Help us nurture it, protect it, and never take it for granted. Let our reconnection be a reflection of Your healing power—a testimony that love, when it is rooted in You, can always find its way back home. Keep our hearts open, our spirits humble, and our connection strong.

In Jesus' name,
Amen

Chapter 7

MY SISTER, MY SHADOW

Honest Truth About Strained Sisterhood and the Journey Toward Peace

*S*isterhood is supposed to mean something soft, safe, and unbreakable. But for me, it's always been more complicated.

I grew up with four sisters—three older than me and one just under me. Two of them I shared a mother with, and I spoke about them in my first memoir. The other two were on my father's side. And while they carried my blood, they never quite carried my heart.

With my older sister on my father's side, we tried to build a relationship. We had moments, small glimpses of connection, but it never stuck. We were different, distant, and despite the effort, it never really worked out. I can't even say we had a falling out because you can't fall out of something that never really began.

My younger sister and I once had a bond. I remember doing her hair, sharing secrets, and laughing over things only sisters would understand. We had a closeness I thought would last, but as she grew older, something shifted. When my father passed away, our connection seemed to pass with him.

I tried to hold on, believing we were stronger than the dysfunction around us. But she started to choose sides, play roles, and repeat patterns I had fought so hard to break free from. That's when I realized I couldn't keep making space for people who only stood with me when it was convenient. I couldn't keep showing up in places where I wasn't seen, valued, or safe. Letting go wasn't easy, but I knew it was necessary.

It hurt to grieve someone who is still alive. It hurt to admit that love wasn't enough to hold us together. But sometimes the most painful part of healing is accepting who can't go with you. For a while, I blamed her. I blamed them. I wondered why they couldn't meet me halfway. Eventually, I saw the truth: we are all on our own journeys, and not everyone is equipped to walk beside you.

Letting go didn't mean I stopped loving them. It meant I started loving myself enough to protect my peace. Sisterhood—real sisterhood—is not about blood. It's about bond, consistency, mutual respect, and love that doesn't shift with the wind.

While I no longer have a relationship with my biological sisters, God, in His goodness, gave me something I never expected: chosen sisters. Two women who love me without conditions, who have cried with me, prayed for me, and spoken life over me. They remind me what sisterhood can be—safe, sacred, and soul-deep. And through them, I've healed.

I no longer look for love where there's only survival. I no longer reach for relationships that refuse to grow. This chapter isn't about blame—it's about release. It's about honoring what was and choosing what will be. Because sisterhood isn't just about what we're born into. It's about what we build.

CLOSING PRAYER

God,

Thank You for clarity in the places where confusion once lived. Thank You for teaching me that not all connections are meant to be forever—and that letting go can be an act of love. I pray for my sisters, both blood and chosen. Bless their paths, soften their hearts, and heal what I couldn't. Thank You for the women You placed in my life to show me what real sisterhood looks like. Help me to always honor them the way You honored me—with love, truth, and grace.

In Jesus' name,
Amen

Chapter 8

BLOOD, SWEAT, AND TEARS—NOW IT'S MY TURN

I Carried Everyone Else – Now I Carry Me

There was a time I would've bled myself dry for the people I loved—and I did. I gave until there was nothing left in me but fragments and fumes. I showed up when I was exhausted, gave love I never received, and poured support into people who wouldn't even hand me a drop of grace when I needed it most. I broke my own heart trying to keep other people whole. And for what? So they could feel safe, seen, and covered—while I stayed in the shadows, depleted and unnoticed.

On every job I've ever had, I was the first one in the office and the last one to leave. I stayed late helping others even after I finished my own work. I went above and beyond because I thought that's what good people do. I believed that if I worked hard enough—if I just stayed consistent, loyal, and dependable—it would count for something. But I learned the hard way that no matter how hard you work, it will never be enough for people who only see you as a body in a chair. I was replaceable. Just another name on a schedule. A resource, not a person.

I worked when I was sick because I was afraid that if I didn't, I'd lose my job. I had leave saved up, but in environments where taking time off was frowned upon, rest felt like a risk I couldn't afford. So I pushed through the pain, the exhaustion, the dizziness, and the stress because showing up seemed safer than slowing down. I carried workloads meant for three people, but I didn't complain or make excuses. I just did what needed to be done, believing that if I kept going, someone would eventually see the effort. Instead, what they saw was someone they could overwork without resistance.

It wasn't until I was completely burned out—mentally, emotionally, physically—that I finally walked away. And that's when they noticed. That's when I heard, "We're going to get you some help." But it was too late. Why did I have to work myself half to death before anyone acknowledged the load I'd been carrying?

And it didn't stop at work. With my family, I gave my all—my time, my energy, my money, and every piece of myself I could offer. I showed up even when it cost me peace. I carried burdens that weren't mine. I became the go-to, the fixer, the strong one, until I was completely exhausted and empty. Still, it wasn't enough. I was loved for what I could give, not for who I was.

The truth is, they never even asked. I just jumped in wherever I saw a need, trying to be everything for everyone. And they let me. They let me carry it all without ever asking how I was holding up. They got comfortable with my self-sacrifice. But the moment I said no—just once—the moment I reminded them of the load I had just carried, the first thing I heard was, "I didn't ask you to do that." And they were absolutely right. They didn't ask. I volunteered. I stepped in before they even had to. But at what point do you stop yourself and say, No thank you, I've got me this time?

That realization gutted me because I saw how I had trained them to expect my yes. I had made myself the solution, the safety net, the emotional first responder. And when I finally needed a break—when I needed someone to notice that I was running on empty—there was no grace, no gratitude. Just a shrug and a reminder that I had done it to myself.

I thought love meant giving everything you had, all the time, without question. But real love doesn't watch you drown in sacrifice and call it loyalty. Real love doesn't leave you empty and then resent you for finally needing to be full.

I gave even when I didn't have it to give. I took out loans. I borrowed from friends just to keep up the façade that I was okay—that I had it all together. I felt like if I wasn't readily available, if I didn't say yes every time, I would be kicked to the curb. And the painful truth is… sometimes I was. People got mad when I said no. They didn't ask why. They didn't care what it cost me. They just saw that I wasn't available for their needs in that moment, and that was enough to make me disposable.

What they didn't know was that when I said no, it wasn't out of spite—it was out of survival. I said no because I truly didn't have it. I was trying to keep myself afloat while pulling others from the water. I was sinking under the weight of trying to be everything for everyone. There were times I gave people money knowing I wouldn't be able to pay my own bills on time. I've handed over my rent money to help someone else—and then held my breath hoping I could somehow make up the difference before my landlord came knocking. I put myself last so often that I forgot what it felt like to be first in my own life.

I gave out of fear—fear of abandonment, fear of being talked about, fear of losing my place in people's lives if I didn't perform. I thought being selfless made me worthy. I thought being needed meant being loved. But all it really did was leave me empty.

And in the process of saving everyone else, I lost the very thing I was trying to protect—my marriage. My husband stopped pouring into our relationship, not because he didn't love me, but because I left him no room to. I was stretched so thin—giving to everyone else—that I had nothing left for him, for us. He stopped trying because I made it seem like I didn't need anything. I had become so consumed with being strong for the world that I forgot how to be soft at home. I forgot how to be vulnerable. I forgot how to receive.

That was one of the hardest truths I had to face—that even my good intentions could cause damage. That overgiving can feel like abandonment to the people closest to you. And it did.

But not anymore. Now, it's my turn.

This chapter of my life isn't about revenge. It's not about payback or bitterness. It's about redirection. All that energy I spent rescuing, fixing, proving, and protecting? I'm finally pouring it back into me. The same way I showed up for others—I'm learning to show up for myself. It's not selfish. It's sacred.

Because nobody sees the wounds beneath the strength. Nobody talks about the women who become the backbones of everything but are never asked if they're okay. We're expected to hold it all together— be the peace, be the answer, be the glue. And we do. Until we break.

I broke. Quietly. Repeatedly. But I also rebuilt. Loudly. Intentionally.

I had to learn how to mother myself. I had to forgive the version of me who thought love meant overextending. I had to grieve the woman I was when I believed my worth was tied to what I could give. Now, I protect my peace like I used to protect other people's feelings. Now, I rest without guilt. Now, I choose me—not just in theory, but in practice.

It took blood, sweat, and tears to keep everyone else afloat. Now it's that same fire—the one that burned me up for others—that's lighting my way forward. I'm using that flame to rebuild, to rise, to walk in my purpose unapologetically.

I don't owe anyone an explanation for my healing. I don't need permission to be whole. I gave away pieces of myself for years, but I'm not doing that anymore.

Now, it's my turn.

TO EVERY WOMAN WHO'S
EVER GIVEN TOO MUCH

If you're reading this and you feel like I'm telling your story—like I just reached into your heart and pulled out your silent pain—I want you to know something: you're not alone. You are not crazy for feeling tired. You are not weak for wanting rest. You are not selfish for needing more than survival.

You've given your blood, sweat, and tears just like I did. You've loved people who didn't know how to love you back. You've shown up for people who couldn't be bothered to notice your absence. You've worked through sickness, smiled through heartbreak, and sacrificed yourself so others could shine. But here's the truth no one ever told us: you matter, too.

You deserve to be poured into, not just poured out. You deserve softness, not just strength. You deserve to be held the way you've held everyone else. It's okay to say no. It's okay to be tired. It's okay to choose you, even if no one else understands.

Let this be the moment you stop shrinking to make others comfortable. Let this be the day you stop apologizing for needing space, love, grace, and rest. You don't have to earn your right to be seen, to be valued, or to be whole. You already are.

So here's to you—the woman who is finally ready to stop bleeding for people who wouldn't even hand her a bandage. Your healing matters. Your peace matters. And your time is now.

With love and truth,
– A Woman Who Finally Chose Herself

CLOSING PRAYER

God,

I've poured out so much—my blood, my sweat, my tears—into people, places, and paths that weren't always meant for me. I gave when I had nothing left. I carried burdens I never should've held. But now, I'm choosing me. Not out of selfishness, but survival.

Not out of pride, but purpose.

Thank You for showing me that my voice matters, my dreams still live, and my turn has finally come. Heal the parts of me that still flinch when I choose myself. Restore what was depleted. Rebuild what was torn. And remind me daily: I am not too late. I am right on time.

In Jesus' name,
Amen

———— ◇◇◇◇◇◇ ————

I FORGIVE YOU (EVEN IF YOU NEVER CHANGE)

*F*orgiveness is not a handshake. It's not always a sit-down conversation or a tearful reunion where both people walk away changed. Sometimes, forgiveness is a quiet decision made in the middle of the night with tears on your pillow and no one there to witness it but God.

I used to think we needed closure to move forward. That reconciliation had to happen in order to heal. But I've come to learn that some people will never understand the damage they caused. Some will never see the pain behind your silence or the cost of their absence.

And so, you have to choose: stay stuck waiting for something that may never come or release it anyway for your own peace.

I forgive you. Not because you asked. Not because you changed. Not because you even acknowledged what you did.

I forgive you because I refuse to carry this weight one more step.

You may never admit how your words shaped me. How your

actions—or your lack of them—cut deep. You may go on thinking you were right, justified, blameless.

But I know the truth. And still, I forgive you.

I forgive you for never saying, "I was wrong." For brushing things under the rug. For pretending everything was okay when it wasn't.

I forgive you for the emotional distance, the unmet needs, the things I begged for that never came. I forgive you for the damage done in silence—the kind of damage that doesn't leave bruises but leaves scars.

I forgive you even if you stay the same. Even if you never see me, never value me, never say the words I waited to hear.

Because forgiveness is not for you. It's for me.

I'm not doing this to keep the peace between us. I'm doing this to keep the peace within myself.

This is not permission to re-enter my life. This is not denial of what you did. This is the boundary, the line in the sand, the healing I gave myself when you refused to give it. You don't have to change. But I did. And I'm not going back.

I forgive you—completely, sincerely, and quietly. Not so we can reconcile, but so I can finally be free. Because the truth is, I cried enough tears to drown in. I held my breath so long, waiting for change, I nearly forgot how to breathe. I've twisted myself in knots trying to be understood by someone who never really wanted to understand me.

I wanted answers. I wanted honesty. I wanted to be met with the same depth I kept giving. But you weren't capable of that, or maybe you just didn't care to be. And I've come to terms with that, too.

What I won't do is keep breaking my own heart trying to reach someone who won't meet me halfway. What I won't do is water myself down hoping it makes me easier to swallow. I'm done bleeding for people who don't even know they're holding a knife.

I forgive you, yes. But that doesn't mean you get to stay.

Forgiveness is mine now. And so is freedom.

REFLECTION

Peace Over People

There comes a moment when you realize that peace is more valuable than presence—especially the presence of people who only bring pain.

I used to think that keeping the peace meant keeping the people. I believed walking away made me disloyal, and choosing silence meant I was wrong. But healing taught me a different truth: peace doesn't come from pretending. It comes from protecting.

I protected my peace when I stopped forcing conversations that always ended in confusion. I protected my peace when I stopped apologizing for my boundaries. I protected my peace when I stopped begging people to see me clearly. And yes, it came at a cost.

There were people I loved that I had to love from a distance. People I used to call family that I now pray for quietly. Relationships I let go of—not because I hated them, but because I finally started loving me.

When I stopped choosing people over peace, my spirit exhaled. I began sleeping through the night. I started laughing without second-guessing the sound. I felt God more clearly because I was no longer surrounded by noise He never sent.

Peace is not passive—it's powerful. And sometimes the most radical thing you can do for your soul is walk away from what once felt familiar but now feels like a battlefield. Not everyone will understand your decision. Some will call you selfish. Some will say you changed. But you can't let that pull you back into places God has already called you out of.

You don't owe explanations for your peace. You don't have to convince people of your growth. You just have to keep walking in it. Because peace is a person. And His name is Jesus. Anything or anyone that costs you Him is simply too expensive.

CLOSING PRAYER

God,

Thank You for being my peace in the absence of people. Thank You for teaching me that letting go isn't failure—it's freedom. Help me to protect what You've healed in me. Strengthen my boundaries. Quiet the voices that guilt me into going backward. Fill every space I clear with Your presence, Your truth, and Your unshakable peace.

In Jesus' Name,
Amen

Chapter 9

---◇◈◇---

WALKING IN MY PROPHETIC CALLING

Owning my spiritual gift, even through fear. How it started showing up

I didn't wake up one day and decide I had a prophetic calling. I wasn't seeking it, chasing it, or even expecting it. Truthfully, I didn't think it had anything to do with me.

It started during a three-night Women's Worth weekend. On the very first night, an elder walked toward me with the kind of authority that made the room go still. She leaned close and said, "God said it's time for you to open your mouth."

Her words hit me like a stone tossed in water—rippling through me, unsettling me.

I smiled politely, but inside I thought, she's got the wrong one. Me? The one with the broken past? The one still trying to figure it out? Surely, God meant someone else.

But that was only the beginning.

That year, I felt the Holy Spirit stirring me. Nudging me to find a church home. I resisted. I made excuses. I said I was fine. But in the quiet, I kept feeling it—an unshakable tug I couldn't explain away.

Eventually, I gave in. I started showing up on Sundays, not every week, but enough to notice that something in me was shifting. Still, I stayed quiet. Still, I questioned. Until the following year—when that same elder found me again.

She locked eyes with me and said, "I see you're still being quiet."

Her words sliced through me. The room fell away. My chest tightened, my throat burned, and for the first time in years, I felt tears spring forward without permission.

That was the day everything changed.

I had been crying out to God silently, begging Him to piece me back together, to heal the parts of me I couldn't even name. And through her prayer that day—deep, spirit-led, heavy with truth—He answered. She prayed things she could not have known. She called out visions I had been too afraid to speak of. She described the sensitivity, the "knowing," the weight I carried but never understood. For the first time, I didn't feel exposed. I felt seen. It was undeniable.

The same silence I had once thought kept me safe was the very silence God was asking me to break. He hadn't been waiting for me to be ready—He had been waiting for me to say yes.

And when I finally surrendered—when I whispered, "Okay, Lord, have Your way"—everything began to align.

The same things I once feared became confirmations. The same voice I used to doubt became the one I trusted most. The same silence that held me captive turned into a stage for obedience.

Now, when I open my mouth, it's not for applause. It's for Him.

I'm still learning. Still stretching. Still surrendering. But this much I know: this gift is not a title I wear—it's an assignment I carry. I am walking in my prophetic calling—slowly, imperfectly, but fully. And the most powerful part? It's not about being heard. It's about being obedient.

"But with every calling comes a choice: which voice will you trust? The one shaped by fear and shame, or the One anchored in peace and truth? That was the next lesson I had to learn—the difference between trauma's echo and God's whisper."

CLOSING PRAYER

God,

Thank You for choosing me even when I questioned my worth. Thank You for every whisper, every nudge, and every confirmation that led me closer to You. Give me boldness to speak what You place in my spirit, and humility to know it's not about me—it's all for Your glory. Quiet my fear, amplify my obedience, and let every word I release be soaked in Your truth and love. Use me as Your vessel, Lord. I surrender my voice to You.

In Jesus' name,
Amen

Chapter 10

◇◈◇

THE VOICE I LEARNED TO TRUST

Distinguishing between trauma, fear, and God's guidance

For most of my life, I didn't know which voice to trust—especially not my own. There was the voice of fear, shaped by trauma, that told me I wasn't good enough, that I would never be more than what I survived. Then there was the voice of shame, whispering that I was too broken, too complicated, too scared to be used by God.

And then there was another voice.

Gentle. Steady. Unlike the others, it didn't come with panic or pressure. It didn't tear me down or rehearse my failures. It didn't shout over my pain—it waited beneath it. God's voice.

It took me years to recognize it. Years of unlearning survival language, of quieting my inner critic, of realizing that just because something sounded urgent didn't mean it was divine. God's voice didn't sound like the ones I grew up hearing. It wasn't harsh or guilt-ridden. It didn't manipulate me into obedience. It loved me into submission. And that love—unshakable, patient, unearned—began to rewire everything I thought I knew.

Learning to hear God meant slowing down. It meant sitting in silence and asking not just, *"What should I do?"* but *"Who do You say I am?"* It meant revisiting old wounds and letting Him speak into them. It meant letting go of people who confused my spirit. It meant risking discomfort for the sake of discernment.

At first, I thought I was losing my mind. But I wasn't losing—I was finally listening. And the more I listened, the more I learned. God's voice brings peace, not confusion. Conviction, not condemnation. Direction, not distraction.

Now, when He speaks, I don't second-guess Him. I've learned to trust that still, small whisper—the one that says, *"Go left,"* when the world says, *"Go right."* The one that says, *"Be still,"* when everything in me wants to run. The one that calls me to speak up when fear begs me to stay silent.

I've followed fear before and it led me straight to chaos. I've followed shame and it led me into hiding. But following God's voice has always led me home—not home in the physical sense, but spiritually. Home to myself. Home to the woman I was always meant to be.

The woman who doesn't flinch when God calls her. The woman who trusts the voice inside her because she knows who placed it there.

There is power in discernment, freedom in clarity, and peace in knowing that God is not the author of confusion—He is the anchor in the storm. I still have moments where I doubt, moments where I ask for confirmation. But I no longer ignore the voice, because I've learned the difference between trauma's echo and truth's whisper.

And that difference is everything.

CLOSING PRAYER

God,

Help me always recognize Your voice—above the noise, above the fear, above the doubt. Teach me to trust what You say, even when it doesn't make sense to anyone else. Help me silence the voices that keep me small and amplify the one that reminds me who I am in You. Thank You for speaking to me—not with force, but with faithfulness. I trust You, Lord. Keep speaking, and I will follow.

In Jesus' name,
Amen

LIVING IN ALIGNMENT

Purpose over performance.
Resting in who God says I am

There was a time when I was always striving—striving to be liked, to be accepted, to be enough. I wore masks just to make others comfortable. I shrank myself to fit into places that couldn't hold the real me. I performed for approval, mistaking it for love.

But performance is exhausting. It drains you while convincing you to clap for your own emptiness. It keeps you chasing validation while losing pieces of your soul in the process. God never asked me to perform. He asked me to align.

Living in alignment isn't about perfection—it's about peace. It's waking up each day and asking, *"Am I walking in the truth of who God created me to be?"* Not who the world expects. Not who my trauma shaped. But the me heaven knows by name. There is a sacred kind of rest that comes when you stop trying to prove your worth and start walking in it.

I had to unlearn a lot to get here. I had to stop clinging to people who only loved the version of me that served them. I had to stop chasing opportunities that were never mine to carry. I had to stop confusing busyness with purpose. Purpose is not loud. It's not performance. It's alignment. It's knowing that even in silence, God is working through you. That even in stillness, there is strength.

Now I don't hustle for validation—I move with identity. I don't strive for perfection—I rest in grace. I know who I am, and more importantly, I know whose I am. Alignment has changed the way I move. I no longer force my way into rooms where God hasn't opened the door. I no longer trade my calling for convenience or approval. I walk with clarity, not compromise.

And yes, I still get tested. Old insecurities still try to creep in. But when they do, I return to the truth: God's voice is steady, and His assignment for me hasn't shifted. I don't need the world to understand it. I just need to walk in it.

Every step I take now is intentional—not because I am chasing, but because I am aligned. And that is freedom.

CLOSING PRAYER

God,

Thank You for showing me the difference between striving and surrender. Thank You for aligning my steps with Your will. Keep me rooted in purpose—not performance. Quiet every voice that tries to pull me out of alignment, and fill me with the confidence to walk in the woman You created me to be. Let peace be my pace. Let truth be my compass. And let Your presence always be enough.

In Jesus' name,
Amen

LETTER TO MY YOUNGER SELF

Dear Younger Me,

I know you're tired. You don't even realize how tired you are yet, but I see it in your eyes—the heaviness you carry, the questions you're too afraid to ask out loud, the ache of wanting to be loved without conditions. I see the little girl who keeps trying to be strong, who hides her pain behind jokes and silence, who keeps showing up even when no one notices.

Let me tell you something no one ever told us: You are not too much. You are not too loud. You are not too sensitive. You are not too broken. You are worthy—right now, exactly as you are.

I know there are things you've been through that no child should ever endure. Nights when you cried into your pillow and no one came. Days when you prayed someone would notice the hurt behind your smile. The chaos wasn't your fault. The neglect wasn't your fault. The pain wasn't your fault. You did the best you could with what you had, and I am so proud of you.

You were never meant to carry it all. But you did. And that makes you brave, even when you felt weak. That makes you resilient, even when you felt broken. That makes you enough, even when the world made you question it.

I want you to know that healing will come—not all at once, and not without scars—but it will come. And you will become the woman you've always dreamed of being. The one who loves herself. The one who sets boundaries. The one who walks away when she's not being valued. The one who forgives but never forgets her worth.

There will be days when you'll still cry, and that's okay. There will be days when the old wounds start to sting, and that's okay, too. But don't ever let that pain convince you that you haven't grown. You are becoming. You are rising. You are everything they said you couldn't be.

So keep going. Even when it's lonely. Even when it's hard. Especially when it's hard. Because one day, you'll look in the mirror and finally see her—the woman who made it, the woman who broke the cycle, the woman who finally figured it out. And you'll smile through the tears because you'll realize she was you all along.

And now, I am her.

With all the love we never knew we deserved,

Future You

Final Interlude

I AM HER NOW

A Triumphant Declaration of Identity, Strength, Grace, and Healing

I am the ending to every curse and the beginning of every promise. I didn't just survive—I became.

I am no longer that scared little girl who cried behind closed doors, wondering if she was enough. I am no longer the woman who begged for love in broken places, trying to prove her worth to people who couldn't see her. I am not defined by what was done to me or by what I had to walk through to make it here.

I am the evidence that healing is real. I am the product of pain turned into power. I am the woman who faced every demon, every lie, every generational curse, and said, *Not anymore. It ends with me.*

I have cried rivers. I have fallen to my knees. I have questioned God and still found Him waiting. I have torn down walls and rebuilt myself with trembling hands and relentless hope. And now—I stand. Not perfect. Not untouched. But whole.

I am her now. The version of me I prayed to become. The one who knows her worth without needing permission. The one who walks away from what no longer serves her, without guilt. The one who understands that softness is strength and grace is power.

I speak truth with a steady voice. I love deeply but not desperately. I protect my peace like it's sacred—because it is. I know now that I don't need validation to be valuable. I understand that boundaries are holy, that healing isn't a destination but a decision I make every day.

I've let go of bitterness. I've forgiven myself for the years I spent lost. I've even found beauty in the parts of me that were once broken. I am her now—the mother who sees, the daughter who overcame, the woman who rose. And I don't owe anyone an explanation for my growth.

I am no longer asking for a seat at any table. I built the table—one where truth, love, and healing are always welcome. So if you ever wonder who I am, don't ask the ones who only knew me in pieces. Ask the woman God put back together.

She'll tell you: I am her now. And I'm never going back.

With fire in my spirit and grace in my bones—

Rhonda Harris

PRAYER REFLECTIONS

Prayer for Strength
Heavenly Father, when the weight of life feels too heavy, remind me that You are my refuge and my strength. When I feel like giving up, be the fire that keeps me going. Strengthen my hands when they tremble, my heart when it's weary, and my spirit when it's broken. Let Your power be made perfect in my weakness. Amen.

Prayer for Peace
Lord, quiet the storms within me. Calm the racing thoughts, the anxious heart, and the restless soul. Replace my worry with Your peace—the kind that surpasses all understanding. Teach me to rest in Your promises, to trust in Your timing, and to breathe deeply in the stillness of Your love. Amen.

Prayer for Forgiveness
Merciful God, help me to forgive—not just others, but also myself. Wash me clean of the guilt I've carried for far too long. Free me from the burden of bitterness and open my heart to release what I cannot change. May I forgive as You have forgiven me—completely, humbly, and without conditions. Amen.

Prayer for Guidance
Father God, when I don't know which way to go, be the voice that whispers, "This is the way." Order my steps, illuminate my path, and close

every door that isn't meant for me. Give me discernment, courage, and wisdom to follow You, even when the road ahead is uncertain. Amen.

Prayer for Gratitude

Lord, thank You for every breath, every blessing, every battle I've survived. Thank You for the lessons hidden in pain and the light that followed every dark season. Thank You for loving me in my mess and molding me in mercy. May I never take Your grace for granted. Amen.

Prayer for Healing

God of Restoration, touch every wound I've carried seen and unseen. Heal the trauma, the heartbreak, the weariness deep in my bones. Restore my joy. Renew my mind. Rebuild what was broken. Let Your healing flow through every part of me and use my story as a testimony of Your power. Amen.

LETTER TO CHIMEEKA— MY FIRST, MY REFLECTION

There are no words strong enough to fully capture the love I have for you—but I'm going to try.

You were the beginning of it all. The one who made me a mother. The one who cracked my heart wide open in the most beautiful way. From the moment I first held you, everything changed. My purpose shifted, my soul awakened, and I knew I had been entrusted with something sacred—you.

Raising you has been one of the greatest joys and greatest lessons of my life. Watching you grow into the woman you are now has been like watching a sunrise slowly stretch across the sky—bold, brilliant, and breathtaking. Your strength humbles me. Your grace moves me. Your spirit lights up any room you walk into.

You are not just my daughter—you are my reflection, my answered prayer, my why. There were moments I didn't think I would make it, but then I'd look at you and remember why I had to keep going. I know we didn't always have it easy. I know there were times you needed more from me and I didn't know how to give it. I may not have had the blueprint, but you gave me reason to build one. And now, I see you building your own for Rosa.

When I watch you with your daughter, I see the cycle breaking. I see the love I gave you being passed down and multiplied. I see healing in motion. I see legacy. You are living proof that the cycle stopped with me and started anew with you. You are an amazing mother, and it brings tears to my eyes to witness the bond you share with Rosa. The way you protect her, guide her, and love her reminds me of the fire that lives in our bloodline. We come from strong women, and you, my daughter, are among the strongest.

Being a mother isn't easy. There are days it will stretch you until you feel like you have nothing left. But you're doing it—and you're doing it well. Never let anyone make you question that. I love you more than every sunrise we've seen and every tear we've cried. I am proud of you—not just for what you've accomplished, but for who you are.

Thank you for choosing to keep showing up. Thank you for being exactly who God made you to be. So keep walking tall, my daughter. Keep breaking, building, and becoming. Because you are everything I prayed for—and more.

With all my heart and everything in me,

Mommy

LETTER TO DAMON—
MY CHOSEN, MY BOND

You came into my life when I least expected it, and from the moment I held you, I knew God had sent me a surprise blessing I didn't even know I needed. You shifted everything—not just my days, but my heart.

You are strong-willed, determined, and unshakable in ways that sometimes leave me speechless. You know what you want. You ask questions that stop me in my tracks. You challenge me, push me, and stretch me in ways no one else ever has. And even though it isn't always easy, I wouldn't trade it for the world—because it reminds me that God trusted me to raise a leader.

You are not afraid to speak your mind, and I love that about you. It tells me you'll never be someone who follows blindly. You'll think. You'll discern. You'll choose what's right for you. That kind of independence can't be taught—it's in you.

But what moves me most about you, DJ, is your heart. It's big. It's tender. It loves deeply. You care about family in a way that's rare, and it reminds me that strength isn't just about being tough—it's about loving with everything you've got.

You've shown me what it means to slow down, to listen, to truly be present. You've reminded me that even as a mother, I'm still learning. I'm still growing. And sometimes, God uses the smallest voices to teach us the biggest lessons.

I know life won't always be easy, but I want you to always remember this: you don't have to carry it all. You don't have to have it all figured out. You don't have to prove your worth to anyone—least of all to me. You already are everything God intended you to be, and my prayer is that you never lose sight of that truth.

I am so proud of you—not just for what you do, but for who you are. Thank you for being my unexpected gift, my daily reminder of grace, and my joy.

With all my love,
Ma

LETTER TO TONY—
MY MIRACLE, MY LEGACY

You are the miracle I never saw coming—but the miracle God always knew I needed.

At 16 years old, I was told I would never bear children. At 24, I suffered a miscarriage that nearly broke me. For years, those words and that loss stayed with me, like a shadow that followed wherever I went. I quietly grieved, quietly carried, quietly wondered if motherhood would forever be something I would long for but never hold.

And then, years after that heartbreak, God rewrote my story. At age 40, I gave birth to you. My miracle. My promise fulfilled. My reminder that He—not doctors, not loss, not statistics—has the final say.

From the moment I first held you, everything in me shifted. You weren't just a baby—you were a living testimony. Proof that prayers don't expire. Proof that restoration is real. Proof that God is always working, even when we can't see it.

Tony, you carry something sacred. A light that can't be dimmed. A strength that feels older than your years. You didn't just arrive in my life—you redeemed it. You gave me purpose in places that once felt hollow. You made me fight harder, believe stronger, love deeper.

I prayed for you before I knew your name. I wept for you before I ever held you. And now that you're here, I will never stop thanking God for the way He chose to write you into my story.

You are my answered prayer. My redemption song. My heartbeat outside of my body

And if you ever wonder how much I love you, just remember this: I survived for you. I changed for you. I live for you. Because you, my son, are living proof that miracles don't just happen—they grow, they smile, they dream, they thrive.

Forever and always,
Mommy

Final Encouragement

*I*f this book found its way into your hands, it's not by accident. It's because God wanted you to know: You're not too far gone. You're not too late. You haven't missed your moment. You are not forgotten.

No matter what you've survived—betrayal, abandonment, dysfunction, silence—you are still standing. And that is not chance. That's grace. That's mercy. That's God refusing to let your story end in pain.

You may not have chosen everything you've walked through, but you do get to choose what you become. You don't have to carry the shame. You don't have to keep proving your worth. You don't have to wait for someone else to say you're enough.

God already did.

If you're still wrestling, still healing, still questioning—good. That means you're still becoming. Healing isn't always loud. Sometimes it looks like rest. Sometimes it feels like silence. But even in the quiet, God is still moving.

So keep showing up for yourself. Keep choosing peace. Keep choosing you. And when it gets hard—and it will—remember this:

A Prayer for You

Heavenly Father, for the one holding these words, I pray for healing. Not just surface healing, but deep, soul-level restoration. Let her know she is seen. Let her feel Your nearness. Where there has been pain, bring purpose. Where there has been silence, bring clarity. Where there has been shame, bring freedom. Remind her she was never meant to carry it all—because You already carried the cross.

Give her courage to walk in truth, strength to let go, and grace to begin again. Let her rise. Let her become. Let her finally live it out.

In Jesus' name, Amen.

You are her now. Don't ever forget it. And don't you dare go back.

With love and fire,
Rhonda Harris

Dear Mama

*I*f I never get the chance to say it loud enough, I want to say it here: thank you.

Thank you for everything you've carried. For everything you've poured into this family. For every silent sacrifice, every whispered prayer, every time you chose strength when no one saw your tears.

You are the reason I know how to show up with love, how to fight with grace, how to keep going even when I'm tired.

I see you now more clearly than I ever have. I feel you in my spirit, in my instincts, in the way I love and protect. I am who I am because of you.

And I want you to know—while you're still here, while I still get to hug you, while I still get to hear your voice—I honor you. Not just for what you've done, but for who you are.

You are my living legacy. My quiet giant. My G.O.A.T.

And I will carry your name, your lessons, and your love with pride for the rest of my life.

I love you. Always.
—Your Granddaughter

Acknowledgments

First and always, I give all glory to God—the Author of my story and the Keeper of my soul. In every moment I thought I was alone, You were there. In every tear I cried in silence, You were listening. In every closed door, detour, or delay, You were protecting me. Thank You for never letting go, even when I tried to let go of myself. This journey, this healing, this testimony—it all belongs to You.

To my incredible husband—thank you for being my steady place. For loving me through the layers, for praying with me, for choosing me even when things felt uncertain. Your unwavering love and quiet strength gave me space to grow and reminded me that peace is possible.

To my children—you are my heart walking outside of my body. Every word I write, every curse I break, every choice to heal—it's for you. Thank you for your grace when I didn't get it right the first time. You are the reason I never gave up.

To my mother—thank you for being the first vessel God used to bring me into this world. Without you, I may never have discovered my passion for reading and writing—gifts that have carried me through my darkest seasons. Our past is layered, but my love for you has always existed—quiet at times, complicated at others, but real through and through. Giving birth to me was enough. And for that alone, I honor you.

To my grandmother—you gave me more than recipes and wisdom. You gave me fire. Before I ever knew how to cover myself in prayer, yours were already wrapped around me. You were strength wrapped in softness, the voice of reason and resilience. Your legacy lives on in every bold step I take, every truth I speak, and every page I write. You didn't just raise a family—you built a foundation. And I'm still standing on it.

To my nephew Kevin—I love you like a son. You inspire me every day, and part of the reason I write is because of you. I'm so proud of the man and author you are. Because of you, Kevin, I write with courage and with love.

Rashad— my nephew, my heart. You carry a strength you don't even see yet. You are braver than your fears, stronger than your battles, and more loved than words could ever hold.

To my favorite uncle—you've driven me crazy more times than I can count, but I wouldn't trade you for the world. Thank you for being the one who always showed up—for loving me loud, making me laugh, and knowing when to push, protect, or simply sit beside me in silence. Your presence has been a constant source of joy, strength, and comfort, and I'm so grateful God made you mine.

To my chosen sisters—you are the family my soul recognized before my mind could understand. You walked into my life not by blood but by divine design. Thank you for seeing me—not just the strong or polished version, but the broken, healing parts too.

Thank you for holding space for me when I couldn't hold it for myself, for being my safe haven in the chaos, and for reminding me I am never alone. You've shown me what real sisterhood looks like—unshakable, unconditional, and unapologetically loyal.

You celebrate my highs, sit with me through my lows, and never let me forget who I am. I may not share your DNA, but I share something deeper—trust, loyalty, and love. And in every way that matters, you are my sisters. Thank you for being the answered prayer I didn't know I was whispering.

To my family and friends—thank you for believing in me when I was too afraid to believe in myself. You can't become your best without first surviving your worst. No matter where this journey leads, I know I'll be okay because I have all of you by my side.

To every mentor, leader, counselor, and prayer warrior who poured into me—your wisdom helped shape the woman I am today.

To every woman reading this—if you've ever been shattered, silenced, overlooked, questioned your worth, carried trauma in silence, or felt unseen—you are not alone. God still has a plan for you. You can rise. You can rebuild. You can walk in purpose.

And finally, to the version of me who didn't quit—you made it. You did the work. You didn't give up. You finally figured it out...and now, you're living it out. I'm proud of you.

With a full heart and a spirit of gratitude—thank you.

Discussion Questions

1. What generational cycles or patterns in your own life do you recognize—and are you ready to break them? How did this memoir help you name what needs healing?

2. Which moment in the author's story did you most identify with—and why? Was there a specific chapter, interlude, or reflection that made you pause and see yourself differently?

3. What does "The Power in My No" mean to you personally? Have you ever struggled with setting boundaries? What would it look like to love yourself more without guilt?

4. The author speaks of rebuilding herself. What parts of your life are you currently rebuilding? What's one area you want to restore with intention and purpose?

5. How has your understanding of family, love, and forgiveness shifted after reading this memoir? Can you hold space for both pain and love in your story like the author did?

6. This memoir talks about healing, but not perfection. What does healing look like for you—right now, in this season? What do you need to give yourself permission to feel or release?

7. What's one lie you believed about yourself that you're ready to let go of? And what truth are you ready to embrace instead?

8. The author's faith journey is deeply woven into her healing. How has your faith (or your view of purpose) grown through your own experiences?

9. The journal entries and reflections were deeply personal. Did they inspire you to start journaling or reflect more honestly with yourself? If so, what would your first journal entry be titled?

10. After finishing this book, what will you do differently in your own life? What is one promise you're making to yourself right now, in this moment?

FINALLY FIGURED IT OUT:
THE SOUNDTRACK

These songs carried me from childhood to womanhood, through heartbreak, healing, and divine purpose. This is the soundtrack of my survival, my becoming, and my breakthrough. Every lyric, every beat, is part of the woman I am today.

Featured Songs Include:

- "Bye Bye" – Mariah Carey
- "Man in the Mirror" – Michael Jackson
- "Imagine Me" – Kirk Franklin
- "He Wasn't Man Enough" – Toni Braxton
- "Silhouette" – Kenny G

...and many more

Scan the QR code or visit the Spotify link to listen.

https://open.spotify.com/playlist/4qesu4aerasbXGbCfR170b?si=e6cbd764cab4471e

UP NEXT WITH RHONDA HARRIS

A look at what's coming beyond *Finally Figured It Out*

Books & Writing
- Growth Hurts: Embracing The Pain
- God Has Now, I Got Next (Waiting & Preparing)
- Follow Your Own Path: Letting Go of Expectations and Walking in Divine Alignment
- Healing the Wound Between Women
- Buried In Loyalty

Journals, Decks & Merch

- 31-DayPrayers for the Journey Journal
- 31-Day Affirmation Deck
- Divine Boldness Candle Collection
- Apparel line (Finally Figured It Out, Born to Stand Out, etc.)

Media & Content

- The Purpose in Pages Podcast (Season 1 launch)
- YouTube Series (God's Compass, When Silence Screams, etc.)

WHAT COMES AFTER BREAKTHROUGH?

You've walked with me through the breaking, the healing, and the becoming.

But the journey doesn't stop here.

UP NEXT

Growth Hurts: Embracing the Pain

A reflective journal of what happens after the silence lifts—when you're finally free… but still figuring out how to live fully.

This is for every woman who's ever asked, "Now what?" after the chains were broken.

Because healing is just the beginning. And yes—growth hurts.

But it's worth every step

About the Author

Rhonda Harris is a storyteller, a truth-teller, and a survivor. In her debut memoir, *Finally Figured It Out: Shattering Generational Curses*, she shares her raw and redemptive journey from brokenness to healing in hopes of inspiring others to rise above their past and walk boldly into their purpose.

With a background in both military and nonprofit service, Rhonda has spent more than a decade supporting those who serve others—first alongside military officials and medical professionals, and later as a Workplace Administrator for a nonprofit. Her passion for people and her gift for encouraging others are central to everything she does.

Rhonda is a proud wife, mother, and grandmother. When she isn't writing or working, you'll find her cooking soulful meals, reading, or enjoying a good movie. She lives with her family in the Washington, D.C. area.

Through every page of her memoir, Rhonda hopes to remind readers that freedom, healing, and peace are possible—no matter where you start.

Thank you for reading *Finally Figured It Out*

If you enjoyed this book, please help spread
the word by leaving an online review.

KEEP IN TOUCH WITH RHONDA HARRIS

Instagram: @ThePurposeInPages
YouTube: The Purpose in Pages
TikTok: @ThePurposeInPages
Facebook: facebook.com/ThePurposeInPages/

www.ingramcontent.com/pod-product-compliance
Lightning Source LLC
Chambersburg PA
CBHW030410130626
46549CB00004B/1711